CISA Exam Prep

550+ Practice Questions

1st Edition

www.versatileread.com

Document Control

Proposal Name	:	CISA Exam Prep: +550 Practice Questions
Document Edition	:	1st
Document Release Date	:	9th May 2024
Reference	:	CISA
VR Product Code	:	20241102CISA

Feedback:

If you have any comments regarding the quality of this book or otherwise alter it to better suit your needs, you can contact us through email at info@versatileread.com

Please make sure to include the book's title and ISBN in your message.

About the Contributors:

Nouman Ahmed Khan

AWS/Azure/GCP-Architect, CCDE, CCIEx5 (R&S, SP, Security, DC, Wireless), CISSP, CISA, CISM, CRISC, ISO27K-LA is a Solution Architect working with a global telecommunication provider. He works with enterprises, mega-projects, and service providers to help them select the best-fit technology solutions. He also works as a consultant to understand customer business processes and helps select an appropriate technology strategy to support business goals. He has more than eighteen years of experience working with global clients. One of his notable experiences was his tenure with a large managed security services provider, where he was responsible for managing the complete MSSP product portfolio. With his extensive knowledge and expertise in various areas of technology, including cloud computing, network infrastructure, security, and risk management, Nouman has become a trusted advisor for his clients.

Abubakar Saeed

Abubakar Saeed is a trailblazer in the realm of technology and innovation. With a rich professional journey spanning over twenty-nine years, Abubakar has seamlessly blended his expertise in engineering with his passion for transformative leadership. Starting humbly at the grassroots level, he has significantly contributed to pioneering the Internet in Pakistan and beyond. Abubakar's multifaceted experience encompasses managing, consulting, designing, and implementing projects, showcasing his versatility as a leader.

His exceptional skills shine in leading businesses, where he champions innovation and transformation. Abubakar stands as a testament to the power of visionary leadership, heading operations, solutions design, and integration. His emphasis on adhering to project timelines and exceeding customer expectations has set him apart as a great leader. With an unwavering commitment to adopting technology for operational simplicity and enhanced efficiency, Abubakar Saeed continues to inspire and drive change in the industry.

Dr. Fahad Abdali

Dr. Fahad Abdali is an esteemed leader with an outstanding twenty-year track record in managing diverse businesses. With a stellar educational background, including a bachelor's degree from the prestigious NED University of Engineers & Technology and a Ph.D. from the University of Karachi, Dr. Abdali epitomizes academic excellence and continuous professional growth.

Dr. Abdali's leadership journey is marked by his unwavering commitment to innovation and his astute understanding of industry dynamics. His ability to navigate intricate challenges has driven growth and nurtured organizational triumph. Driven by a passion for excellence, he stands as a beacon of inspiration within the business realm. With his remarkable leadership skills, Dr. Fahad Abdali continues to steer businesses toward unprecedented success, making him a true embodiment of a great leader.

Muniza Kamran

Muniza Kamran is a technical content developer in a professional field. She crafts clear and informative content that simplifies complex technical concepts for diverse audiences, with a passion for technology. Her expertise lies in Microsoft, cybersecurity, cloud security and emerging technologies, making her a valuable asset in the tech industry. Her dedication to quality and accuracy ensures that her writing empowers readers with valuable insights and knowledge. She has done certification in SQL database, database design, cloud solution architecture, and NDG Linux unhatched from CISCO.

Table of Contents

About CISA Certification

Introduction

This section provides an overview of the CISA (Certified Information Systems Auditor) certification, emphasizing its significance in the field of IT audit, control, and security. It highlights the benefits of obtaining CISA certification, outlines the certification process, and discusses the importance of adhering to professional ethics. Additionally, it explores the demand for CISA-certified professionals in the evolving cybersecurity landscape, setting the stage for further discussion on exam preparation and career opportunities.

What is a CISA?

This is a globally recognized IT audit, control, and security professional designation. CISAs are qualified to assess an organization's IT systems and controls, identify vulnerabilities, and report on compliance. To become a CISA, individuals must pass a comprehensive exam and meet the experience requirements set by ISACA, the Information Systems Audit and Control Association [ISACA CISA Certification].

Benefits of CISA

Obtaining a CISA (Certified Information Systems Auditor) certification offers numerous benefits to information systems audit, control, and security professionals. Firstly, it significantly enhances career opportunities by opening doors to a wide range of job roles and advancement prospects. Employers highly seek certified individuals due to their demonstrated expertise and credibility in assessing vulnerabilities, implementing controls, and ensuring compliance within organizations' information systems. Additionally, CISA certification often results in increased earning potential, with certified professionals commanding higher salaries compared to their non-certified counterparts. Moreover, CISA is globally recognized, providing credibility and recognition to certified individuals across international job markets. It also fosters professional development by requiring rigorous study and examination, ensuring that certified professionals stay updated with the latest trends, technologies, and best practices in the field. Furthermore, CISA certification is endorsed by ISACA (Information Systems Audit and Control Association), a leading professional association, further solidifying its industry recognition and credibility. Overall, CISA certification offers a pathway to career advancement, increased earning potential, industry recognition, and professional development, making it a valuable investment for information systems audit and security professionals.

The CISA Certification Process

The CISA (Certified Information Systems Auditor) certification process typically involves several steps:

1. **Meet Eligibility Requirements**: Candidates must meet specific eligibility requirements set by ISACA, which typically include a minimum level of education and work experience in information systems auditing, control, assurance, or security. As of the last update, the eligibility criteria include a minimum of five years of professional work experience in information systems auditing, control, or security.

2. **Register for the Exam:** Once eligible, candidates can register for the CISA exam through the ISACA website. The exam is administered globally at designated testing centers.

3. **Prepare for the Exam:** Candidates typically prepare for the CISA exam by studying relevant materials, such as ISACA's official CISA Review Manual, attending training courses, or using other study resources available through ISACA or third-party providers.

4. **Pass the Exam:** The CISA exam consists of multiple-choice questions covering various information systems auditing, control, and security domains. Candidates must pass the exam to proceed to the next step.

5. **Apply for Certification:** After passing the exam, candidates must apply for CISA certification to ISACA. This application includes details of the candidate's education, work experience, and adherence to the ISACA Code of Professional Ethics.

6. **Adherence to Continuing Professional Education (CPE) Requirements:** Certified individuals must adhere to ISACA's Continuing Professional Education (CPE) requirements to maintain their certification. This involves completing a specified number of CPE hours annually to stay up-to-date with developments in the field.

Experience Requirements

Regarding the experience required for CISA certification, candidates must have a minimum of five years of professional work experience in information systems auditing, control, or security. This experience should be gained within the ten years preceding the application for certification or within five years of passing the exam. Additionally, a maximum of one year of experience waivers or substitutions may be available for certain education or work experience qualifications. It's essential for candidates to carefully review and ensure they meet the eligibility requirements set by ISACA before applying for CISA certification.

ISACA Codes of Professional Ethics

The ISACA (Information Systems Audit and Control Association) Code of Professional Ethics serves as a guiding framework for members, including those holding certifications like CISA (Certified Information Systems Auditor), outlining fundamental principles to uphold professional integrity and ethical conduct. Firstly, members are encouraged to actively contribute to the professional community by sharing knowledge, supporting development, and maintaining the reputation of the profession. Integrity is paramount, requiring members to act honestly, responsibly, and ethically, avoiding conflicts of interest and preserving confidentiality. Continuous professional development is emphasized, mandating members to stay abreast of industry trends and enhance their skills. Upholding confidentiality is also stressed, necessitating the protection of sensitive information and privacy rights. Adherence to these principles is crucial for maintaining the credibility and trustworthiness of the profession, and failure to comply may result in disciplinary action by ISACA. Thus, ISACA members, including CISA-certified professionals, must adhere to the Code of Professional Ethics throughout their careers to ensure ethical behavior and uphold the standards of the profession.

ISACA Standards

ISACA (Information Systems Audit and Control Association) does not develop standards in the same way that organizations like ISO (International Organization for Standardization) do. Instead, ISACA provides guidance, frameworks, and best practices related to information systems audit, control, and governance. Some of the well-known frameworks and guidance documents developed by ISACA include:

- **COBIT (Control Objectives for Information and Related Technologies):** COBIT is a widely recognized framework for the governance and management of enterprise IT. It provides a comprehensive set of controls, processes, and best practices to help organizations align IT with business objectives, manage risks, and ensure compliance.
- **IT Assurance Framework (ITAF):** ITAF guides conducting information systems audits and assurance engagements. It outlines principles, standards, and practices for planning, executing, and reporting on various IT audits, including financial, compliance, and performance audits.
- **Risk IT Framework:** The Risk IT Framework offers guidance on managing IT-related risks effectively. It helps organizations identify, assess, and mitigate IT risks in alignment with business objectives and risk appetite.
- **Cybersecurity Nexus (CSX):** CSX provides resources and guidance for cybersecurity professionals, including training, certifications, and knowledge resources to help address the evolving challenges of cybersecurity.

The Certification Exam

The CISA (Certified Information Systems Auditor) certification exam is a comprehensive assessment designed to evaluate candidates' knowledge and expertise in information systems audit, control, and security. Here are some key aspects of the CISA certification exam:

- **Format:** The CISA exam typically consists of multiple-choice questions that assess candidates' understanding of various domains related to information systems auditing, control, and security. The exam format may include single-answer and multiple-answer questions.
- **Domains:** The exam covers five domains, each representing a different aspect of information systems auditing and control. These domains include:
    - Domain 1: Information System Auditing Process
    - Domain 2: Governance and Management of IT
    - Domain 3: Information Systems Acquisition, Development, and Implementation
    - Domain 4: Information Systems Operations, Maintenance, and Support
    - Domain 5: Protection of Information Assets
- **Content Coverage**: The exam assesses candidates' knowledge and understanding of key concepts, principles, best practices, and techniques related to each domain. Topics covered include risk management, IT governance, information security, compliance, and more.
- **Duration:** The exam duration is typically four hours. Candidates must manage their time effectively to complete all sections of the exam within the allotted time frame.
- **Passing Score:** The passing score for the CISA exam is determined through a psychometrically sound process and may vary from one administration to another. Candidates receive their scores immediately upon completing the exam.
- **Preparation:** Candidates are encouraged to prepare thoroughly for the exam by studying relevant materials, such as the official CISA Review Manual, attending training courses, and using practice exams and study guides.
- **Administration:** The CISA exam is administered by ISACA and is offered at designated testing centers worldwide. Candidates must

register for the exam through the ISACA website and select a convenient testing location and date.

Exam Information

Certified Information Systems Auditor

Prior Certification		Exam Validity	
Not Required		**12 Months**	
Exam Fee		Exam Duration	
$575 USD/Members **$760 USD/ Non-Members**		**240 Minutes**	
No. of Questions		Passing Marks	
150 Questions		**450/800**	

Recommended Experience

Minimum of 5 years of experience in IS/IT audit, assurance, control, or security

Exam Format

Multiple Choice Questions

Languages

French, German, Chinese Traditional, Chinese Simplified, Hebrew, Japanese, Italian, Turkish, Spanish, Korean and Portuguese Other than English

Exam Preparation

Before Exam

Prior to the exam, it's crucial to establish a solid study plan to manage time and cover all necessary materials effectively. Gathering relevant study resources, such as the official CISA Review Manual and practice exams, is essential for comprehensive preparation. Practice exams help familiarize oneself with the exam format and identify areas for improvement. Additionally, focusing on understanding key concepts rather than rote memorization is key. Taking care of physical and mental well-being by maintaining a healthy lifestyle and avoiding last-minute cramming is important for optimal performance.

Day of exam

On the day of the exam, arriving early at the testing center ensures ample time for check-in procedures and settling nerves. Bringing all necessary items, including identification and exam admission tickets, is vital. Maintaining a calm and focused mindset throughout the exam is essential, ensuring careful reading of each question and thoughtful responses. Time management is crucial, allowing adequate time for each question and a final review before submission. Above all, maintaining a positive attitude and confidence in one's preparation can significantly contribute to success on exam day.

After Exam

After completing the exam, take time to reflect on the experience, analyzing both strengths and weaknesses. It's essential to relax and unwind, allowing oneself to recharge. For those who passed, congratulations are in order, and future steps may include considering additional certifications or focusing on professional development. For those who didn't pass, it's crucial not to lose heart but instead view the experience as an opportunity for growth. Planning for a retake with renewed focus and determination is the key.

Retaining your Certified Information Systems Auditor (CISA)

Retaining your Certified Information Systems Auditor (CISA) certification involves fulfilling certain requirements set by ISACA (Information Systems Audit and Control Association) to ensure that certified professionals remain competent and up-to-date in the field of information systems auditing and control. Here are the key steps to retain your CISA certification:

Continuing Education

CISA certification holders are required to earn a specified number of Continuing Professional Education (CPE) hours annually to maintain their certification. CPE activities may include attending training courses, workshops, conferences, and webinars or completing self-study programs related to information systems auditing, control, and security. ISACA guides the types of activities that qualify for CPE credits and how to report them.

CPE Maintenance Fees

- Certified professionals must accurately report their CPE activities to ISACA through the online CPE reporting system. This includes providing details such as the activity title, date, duration, and the number of CPE hours earned. ISACA may conduct random audits to verify CPE compliance, so it's essential to maintain records of all completed activities.
- CISA certification holders are required to pay annual maintenance fees to ISACA to retain their certification. These fees support ISACA's ongoing operations and initiatives, including the development of new certifications, resources, and professional development opportunities for members.

Revocation of Certificate

The revocation of a Certified Information Systems Auditor (CISA) certificate is a consequential action taken by the Information Systems Audit and Control Association (ISACA) in response to serious violations or misconduct by certificate holders. Instances that may lead to revocation include ethical breaches, criminal convictions related to the practice of information systems auditing, misrepresentation of qualifications, failure to meet certification requirements, or professional misconduct. Such actions undermine the integrity of the profession and jeopardize the interests of clients, employers, and the public. ISACA follows a formal disciplinary process, which includes investigation, hearings, and appeals, before deciding to revoke a certificate. Revocation of a CISA certificate carries significant repercussions for the individual's career and professional reputation, emphasizing the importance of upholding ethical standards and compliance with certification requirements in the field of information systems auditing and control.

CISA Exam Preparation Pointers

Preparing for the CISA (Certified Information Systems Auditor) exam requires careful planning and dedication. Here are some pointers to help you effectively prepare for the exam:

- Familiarize yourself with the exam domains and content outline provided by ISACA. The CISA exam typically covers five domains: Information System Auditing Process, Governance and Management of IT, Information Systems Acquisition, Development and Implementation, Information Systems Operations, Maintenance and Support, and Protection of Information Assets.
- Utilize official study materials provided by ISACA, such as the CISA Review Manual and CISA Review Questions, Answers & Explanations Database. These resources are specifically designed to help candidates understand the exam content and structure.
- Practice exams are invaluable tools for assessing your knowledge and readiness for the exam. Use ISACA's online practice exams or other reputable resources to simulate exam conditions and identify areas for improvement.
- Develop a study plan that outlines what topics you need to cover and how much time you'll dedicate to each. Be consistent and realistic in your study schedule, allowing for regular review and practice sessions.
- Identify areas where you feel less confident and allocate extra time to review and practice those topics. Use study aids online resources, or seek clarification from experienced professionals if needed.
- Keep abreast of the latest developments, trends, and best practices in information systems auditing and control. Subscribe to relevant newsletters, blogs, or professional associations to stay informed.

- Consider joining study groups or forums where you can collaborate with other candidates, share study tips, and discuss challenging topics. Peer support can be motivating and beneficial during the exam preparation process.
- Practice effective time management during practice exams and study sessions to ensure you can complete all questions within the allotted time during the actual exam.
- Maintain a healthy lifestyle, get enough sleep, and manage stress effectively during the exam preparation period. Taking care of your physical and mental well-being will help you stay focused and perform your best on exam day.
- Familiarize yourself with ISACA's exam policies and procedures, including rules regarding calculators, identification requirements, and exam day logistics. Being well-prepared and informed will help alleviate any unnecessary stress on exam day.

Job Opportunities with CISA Certifications

Roles of CISA-Certified Professionals:

Compliance Analyst

These professionals ensure that organizations adhere to relevant data security regulations and industry standards. CISA certification demonstrates expertise in compliance frameworks.

Risk Analyst

This role involves identifying and mitigating potential risks to information systems. The CISA curriculum equips you with risk assessment skills.

Information Security Manager

These managers oversee the implementation and maintenance of IT security protocols. A CISA certification showcases your understanding of security best practices.

IT Auditor

Responsible for evaluating the effectiveness of an organization's IT controls, a CISA certification makes you a strong candidate for this role.

Data Protection Manager

This role focuses on safeguarding sensitive data. Your CISA knowledge helps identify such data and ensure proper controls are in place.

Demand for CISA Certification in 2024

The demand for CISA (Certified Information Systems Auditor) certification is expected to remain high in 2024

- **Growing reliance on digital infrastructure:** Organizations are increasingly dependent on technology, making robust IT security crucial. CISA professionals ensure these systems are audited and secured.
- **Escalating cyber threats:** Cyberattacks are on the rise, and businesses need qualified personnel to identify vulnerabilities and implement safeguards. CISA certification validates expertise in this area.
- **Evolving cybersecurity landscape:** The cybersecurity domain is constantly changing. The CISA certification process is designed to keep professionals updated on the latest threats and technologies.

Practice Questions

1. What event triggered the creation of ISO 15489 as the new standard of records management worldwide?

A. The Enron scandal
B. The Madoff Ponzi scheme
C. The WorldCom scandal
D. Italy's Parmalat Dairy Scandal

2. Which company's actions led to the formation of the US Sarbanes-Oxley Act, a corporate governance law for internal controls?

A. AIG
B. WorldCom
C. Tyco International
D. Goldman Sachs

3. What was the nature of the charges that John M. Cinderey of United Commercial Bank settled with the SEC?

A. Insider trading
B. Falsifying loan loss records
C. Bribery and racketeering
D. Overstating income and reserves

4. What is the primary purpose of introducing new regulations according to the text?

A. To increase corporate profits
B. To eliminate executive choice
C. To prevent shortcuts and ensure control
D. To simplify legal compliance

5. Which act is similar to the US government's internal controls in the Office of Management and Budget Circular A-123?

A. US Sarbanes-Oxley Act (SOX)
B. Federal Financial Institutions Examination Council (FFIEC)

C. Basel Accord

D. Health Insurance Portability and Accountability Act (HIPAA)

6. Which of the following is not a banking regulation mentioned in the text?

A. Payment Card Industry (PCI) Data Security Standard

B. Basel Accord

C. Federal Information Security Management Act (FISMA)

D. Gramm-Leach-Bliley Financial Services Modernization Act

7. What does the Payment Card Industry (PCI) Security Standards Council oversee?

A. Data Security Standard for credit processing

B. Internal controls for publicly traded corporations

C. Security of government information processing

D. International financial reporting standards

8. What does an IS auditor verify regarding assets, threats, and vulnerabilities?

A. That they are properly insured

B. That they are patented and trademarked

C. That they are properly identified and managed to reduce risk

D. That they are updated in the company's financial statements

9. Which of the following is not a type of data described in the text?

A. Data content

B. Authentication data

C. Metadata

D. Encrypted data

10. What is the fundamental objective of all regulations mentioned in the text?

A. To decrease operational costs

B. To protect valuable assets and ensure operational integrity

C. To increase transparency for investors

D. To enhance international trade agreements

11. What is the primary purpose of a policy in an organization?

A. To provide step-by-step instructions
B. To identify a topic of concern and risks to avoid or prevent
C. To specify a standard containing a list of specific measurement points
D. To provide general instructions for unusual occasions

12. What indicates an executive control failure within an organization?

A. A standard that is too detailed
B. A missing procedure
C. A missing policy
D. A guideline that is too vague

13. What is the role of standards in an organization?

A. To provide a work flow of specific tasks
B. To identify specific control points necessary for compliance
C. To give general advice on achieving organizational objectives
D. To mandate the objectives and responsible parties

14. Which type of standard is mandated by a government law or agency?

A. Regulatory Standard
B. Industry Standard
C. Organizational Standard
D. Personal Standard

15. What is true about guidelines in an organization?

A. They are mandatory for compliance
B. They provide specific step-by-step instructions
C. They are used to define requirements
D. They are discretionary and usually incomplete

16. What are procedures designed to achieve?

A. To set high-level goals
B. To maintain the highest possible control over outcomes

C. To suggest possible actions for future standards

D. To provide emphasis and set the direction for tasks

17. What does the lack of written procedures in an organization indicate?

A. Innovation and flexibility

B. Dereliction of duty

C. Efficient management

D. Robust guidelines

18. Who typically issues policies that receive widespread support within an organization?

A. Subordinate employees

B. Elected officials and upper management

C. External consultants

D. All employees equally

19. What should auditors focus on to identify high-risk activities?

A. The most commonly used procedures

B. The policies signed by lower-level managers

C. High-risk activities and seldom-used procedures

D. The guidelines provided for everyday situations

20. What is the primary objective of ISACA's code of ethics for certified IS auditors?

A. To maximize personal gains from audits

B. To protect the auditors' interests only

C. To ensure the implementation of appropriate information systems policies and procedures

D. To minimize the workload of auditors

21. What should auditors do with confidential information obtained during an audit?

A. Share it with other clients to help them improve

B. Use it for personal benefit

C. Maintain privacy and confidentiality except for required legal disclosure

D. Sell the information to the highest bidder

22. What may happen if a CISA fails to comply with the code of professional ethics?

A. They may receive a warning
B. They may be promoted for being practical
C. They may be subject to an investigation and possible sanctions
D. They will receive no consequences

23. Which of the following behaviors is considered unethical and could result in the forfeiture of professional certifications?

A. Attending professional development courses
B. Reporting all audit findings accurately
C. Theft of intellectual property
D. Maintaining confidentiality

24. What is the expectation for auditors in terms of professional competency?

A. Auditors should only undertake activities for which they are professionally competent
B. Auditors should rely solely on technically qualified specialists
C. Auditors should focus only on areas where they can improve their competency
D. Auditors should delegate all complex tasks to others

25. What could be the consequence of failing to report violations promptly?

A. A promotion for discretion
B. Amnesty for the reporter
C. Amnesty for those who report the violation after the reporter
D. No consequences at all

26. Why is it important for auditors to admit mistakes?

A. To avoid legal repercussions
B. To compound and worsen the problem
C. To maintain honesty and allow for resolution
D. To shift blame to others

27. How do auditors contribute to the ongoing education of stakeholders?

A. By taking responsibility for fixing problems

B. By facilitating the use of control self-assessment (CSA)

C. By sharing confidential information as learning material

D. By offering personal opinions on security matters

28. According to ISACA's code of ethics, what is an auditor's duty when findings are discovered?

A. To fix the problems immediately

B. To ignore minor issues

C. To report the finding and whether it has been fixed

D. To only report issues that are beneficial to the auditor

29. What is the ISACA code of ethics stance on auditors using audit information for personal benefit?

A. It is encouraged if it leads to better audit practices

B. It is allowed for educational purposes

C. It is strictly prohibited

D. It is acceptable if it does not harm the client

30. What is the primary goal of an audit?

A. To improve the business model

B. To check compliance with financial records

C. To determine the truth based on evidence

D. To assist staff in improving their performance

31. What type of audit involves auditors within their organization?

A. Internal Audits

B. External Audits

C. Independent Audits

D. Compliance Audits

32. Which type of audits are performed by third-party auditors for licensing, certification, or product approval?

A. Internal Audits

B. External Audits

C. Independent Audits

D. Compliance Audits

33. What kind of audits verify whether the activities or sequence of activities meet the published requirements?

A. Product Audits

B. Process Audits

C. System Audits

D. Operational Audits

34. Which ISO standard is associated with quality management?

A. ISO 27001

B. ISO 9001

C. ISO 15489

D. ISO 31000

35. What do system audits primarily focus on evaluating?

A. Product attributes

B. Financial records

C. Management of the system including its configuration

D. Efficiency of operational practices

36. What is the purpose of a compliance audit?

A. To verify internal policies and procedures

B. To check the integrity of financial records

C. To verify the implementation of and adherence to a standard or regulation

D. To assess the value of the organization's assets

37. During which type of audit are routine checkups conducted between certification and recertification audits?

A. Surveillance Audits

B. Integrated Audits

C. Financial Audits

D. Administrative Audits

38. What differentiates an audit from an assessment?

A. Audits are less formal than assessments
B. Audits are conducted by internal staff, while assessments are external
C. Audits must be both objective and impartial, while assessments are more cooperative
D. Assessments have a higher assurance of truth than audits

39. What is the responsibility of an auditor in their fiduciary relationship?

A. To put the auditee's interests ahead of the truth
B. To act for the benefit of another person, placing fairness and honesty above their interests
C. To guide the organization to pass an external audit
D. To assist in product development and design specifications

40. What are the two primary roles directly involved in an audit?

A. Client and Auditor
B. Auditee and Client
C. Auditor and Lead Auditor
D. Auditor and Auditee

41. Who may assume the role of a client in an audit context?

A. External customer only
B. Internal audit department only
C. Regulatory group only
D. Audit committee, external customer, internal audit department, or regulatory group

42. What is a critical requirement for an auditor to maintain during an audit?

A. Financial gain
B. Independence
C. Organizational relationship with the auditee
D. Participation in design decisions

43. What is the consequence of an auditor not being independent?

A. The audit can proceed as usual.
B. The audit findings may lack objectivity and are doubtful.
C. The auditor receives a reward.
D. The audit is considered more reliable.

44. What should an auditor do if they are not independent?

A. Proceed with the audit without mentioning it.
B. Receive a gift of value to compensate.
C. Disclose the conflict immediately to the lead auditor.
D. Provide design advice to the auditee.

45. What is the outcome for an auditor who becomes involved in the auditee's design decisions?

A. They are promoted.
B. They are disqualified from auditing any related work.
C. They are given a financial bonus.
D. They become part of the auditee's staff.

46. According to the text, what is the truth for an auditor?

A. The truth is subjective.
B. The truth is negotiable.
C. The truth is the truth until you add to it.
D. The truth depends on the auditee's perspective.

47. What should an auditor avoid doing during their role?

A. Reporting findings
B. Asking questions
C. Participating in remediation
D. Maintaining records

48. What can happen if an auditor provides design advice while engaged as an external auditor?

A. They are seen as more helpful.
B. They lose their independence and objectivity.

C. They become more integral to the auditee.

D. Their findings are deemed more accurate.

49. What is an auditor's responsibility under various auditing standards?

A. To ensure financial gain

B. To maintain a close relationship with the auditee

C. To report findings that are fair and objective

D. To participate in the auditee's decision-making process

50. What is the primary function of the Sarbanes-Oxley Act (SOX)?

A. To govern risk reduction in banking.

B. To enforce information security requirements for merchants.

C. To mandate full disclosure of potential control weaknesses to the audit committee.

D. To set maximum service outages for basic account functions.

51. What type of actions in regulations are indicated by the word "shall"?

A. Discretionary actions.

B. Mandatory actions.

C. Suggested actions.

D. Informal recommendations.

52. Which standard is responsible for the measurement of products by attributes?

A. COSO

B. OECD

C. ISO

D. PCAOB

53. According to ISACA standards, what does the audit charter (standard 1001) document?

A. The independence of the auditor.

B. The proficiency of the auditor.

C. The scope and purpose of the audit.

D. The criteria for the audit.

54. What is the focus of the Basel Accord Standard III?

A. Privacy in healthcare organizations.
B. Risk management controls in banking.
C. Security requirements for merchants.
D. Information security for government systems.

55. What is the main goal of financial audits according to the text?

A. To protect the stock market.
B. To hold executives accountable for the accuracy of financial reports.
C. To ensure compliance with IT-specific controls.
D. To promote standardization in multinational business.

56. What does the term "materiality" refer to in ISACA's audit standard 1204?

A. The independence of the auditor.
B. The evidence that portrays the most accurate story.
C. The planning of engagement.
D. The use of other experts' work.

57. What is the purpose of the US Gramm-Leach-Bliley Act (GLBA)?

A. To mandate risk management controls in banking.
B. To set standards for financial audits.
C. To set maximum service outages for account functions and mandate public disclosure of security breaches.
D. To enforce data protection controls in banking.

58. According to the text, who is ultimately responsible for ensuring financial integrity in an organization?

A. The IS auditors.
B. The corporate officers.
C. The IT department.
D. The regulatory bodies.

59. What is the primary indicator of the health of a business according to executive management?

A. Operating Costs

B. Current Sales

C. Revenue Opportunity

D. Compliance with regulations

60. What is the concept of 'least privilege' in the context of an auditor's responsibility?

A. Sharing all information with the management

B. Providing complete access to all company records

C. Providing only the minimum information necessary to complete a task

D. Granting access to all employees for transparency

61. What should auditors do to maintain confidentiality of sensitive information?

A. Discuss the information with legal counsel

B. Leave all records in the custody of the client

C. Store all documents in a personal safe

D. Share information with team members only

62. Who should hire the auditor for legal confidentiality under attorney-client privilege to be potentially applicable?

A. The auditors themselves

B. The client's lawyer

C. The client directly

D. A third-party agency

63. What is the recommended attire for auditors according to the text?

A. Casual wear

B. Same as the client's attire

C. More formal than the client's attire

D. Athletic wear

64. Which of the following is not a characteristic of good leadership as described in the text?

A. Demanding compliance without feedback
B. Developing specific requirements for success
C. Paying attention to comments and complaints
D. Taking criticism and educating staff

65. What should an auditor do when they lack evidence of acceptable quantity, relevance, and reliability?

A. Make assumptions based on experience
B. Use evidence from previous audits
C. Formulate an opinion based on intuition
D. Render a score based on the evidence captured

66. What is the primary concern of IT supporting roles?

A. Designing the security architecture
B. Purchasing, installing, and supporting products
C. Writing software applications
D. Protecting against zero-day attacks

67. What is the standard retention period for audit documentation?

A. 3 years
B. 5 years
C. 7 years
D. 10 years

68. Which of the following is not a recommended practice for auditors to alleviate fear and anxiety in clients?

A. Establish mutual respect
B. Place blame on specific individuals for problems
C. Establish a mutual understanding of the auditor's role
D. Simplify explanations for the auditee

69. What is the primary focus of the CEO in a corporate organizational structure?

A. Managing daily operations
B. Generating revenue for the organization

C. Overseeing financial controls

D. Directing human resources

70. Who has full authority over all officers and executives in a corporate organizational structure?

A. CEO

B. CFO

C. Audit and Oversight Committee

D. Board of Directors

71. To whom does the Chief Information Officer (CIO) usually report?

A. CEO

B. COO

C. CFO

D. Board of Directors

72. In a corporate organizational structure, which role is equivalent to a divisional president or vice president in a consulting firm?

A. Managing Partner

B. Partner

C. Engagement Manager

D. Senior Consultant

73. Which position in a corporate organizational structure is dedicated to increasing the revenue generated by the business?

A. CEO

B. COO

C. CFO

D. CIO

74. Who in a corporate organizational structure is usually liable to government prosecutors?

A. Staff Workers

B. Department Directors

C. Vice Presidents

D. Consultants

75. What is the role of an Engagement Manager in a consulting firm?

A. Generating revenue for the organization

B. Managing the client relationship and audit execution

C. Providing daily supervision to staff

D. Performing lower-level administrative tasks

76. After how many full audits can a Systems Analyst/Entry-Level Auditor move up to an Auditor/Consultant role according to ISO 27006 audit standard?

A. After at least one full audit

B. After at least two full audits

C. After at least three full audits

D. After at least four full audits

77. Who is responsible for controls over capital and other areas like financial accounting, human resources, and information systems in a corporate organizational structure?

A. CEO

B. COO

C. CFO

D. CIO

78. In a corporate organizational structure, which role is responsible for the professional development of the staff in a consulting firm?

A. Managing Partner

B. Partner

C. Engagement Manager

D. Senior Consultant

79. According to the text, which of the following is NOT a high-level management objective to be verified by the auditor?

A. A strategic alignment between IT and the enterprise objectives

B. A process of monitoring assurance practices for executive management

C. An intervention to stop, modify, or fix failures as they occur

D. Implementation of the most advanced technology in the industry

80. What is the main purpose of corporate governance as defined by ISACA?

A. To create the most elaborate and systematic plan of action

B. To dictate technical details in the IT steering committee

C. To ensure the ethical behavior of corporate executives towards shareholders and stakeholders

D. To guarantee the personal success of the CEO

81. What is the role of an IT steering committee in an organization?

A. To directly manage daily IT operations

B. To convey current business requirements from business executives to the IT executive

C. To implement IT systems without consulting business units

D. To reduce the IT department's influence on business decisions

82. According to Claude Hopkins, What critical factor is necessary for a hamburger business to succeed?

A. A secret recipe

B. Location of the business

C. Finding hungry customers

D. The efficiency of staff

83. Which of the following is NOT one of the perspectives included in the Balanced Scorecard (BSC) methodology?

A. Customer

B. Financial

C. Growth & Learning

D. Competitive Analysis

84. Which project management credential is recognized for providing a complete workflow and is NOT theory-only?

A. Project Management Professional (PMP)
B. Certified Associate in Project Management (CAPM)
C. PRINCE2 Practitioner
D. Agile Certified Practitioner (ACP)

85. What fundamentally changes when an organization implements the Balanced Scorecard?

A. The organization's mission statement
B. How employees prioritize and report their work
C. The organization's market share
D. The technology used by the organization

86. What is the primary mechanism for ensuring IT alignment in an organization?

A. IT department's discretion
B. Implementation of the most sophisticated IT systems
C. An IT steering committee
D. A directive from the legal department

87. What action is necessary for governance to exist when a company outsources services?

A. Reducing the number of stakeholders
B. Increasing the budget for outsourced services
C. Having a right to audit the service provider
D. Delegating all responsibilities to the service provider

88. In the context of the provided text, what is the role of a Project Management Office (PMO)?

A. To handle daily IT operations
B. To provide centralized reporting and support for project management activities
C. To take direct charge of executing projects
D. To regulate the organization's investment portfolio

89. What is the primary goal of tactical management within an organization?

A. To hire new employees
B. To manage the return on investment for information systems
C. To create strategic plans
D. To redesign the organizational structure

90. What do performance metrics help to determine in tactical management?

A. The number of employees in an organization
B. The effectiveness of marketing campaigns
C. Whether results are improving or deteriorating against a baseline
D. The stock prices of the company

91. Who is responsible for providing support to strategic objectives at the tactical level?

A. Entry-level employees
B. Managers
C. Directors
D. Top management

92. What type of planning work is primarily accomplished at the director level?

A. Strategic planning
B. Tactical planning
C. Operational planning
D. Contingency planning

93. From where are strategic plans handed down to the director level?

A. Middle management
B. Top management
C. External consultants
D. Shareholders

94. What is expected of directors at the tactical level?

A. To create their strategic plans
B. To fulfill the strategic goals by providing solutions
C. To make changes in the organizational structure
D. To manage day-to-day operations of all departments

95. What is the extent of a director's authority outside their department?

A. Unlimited authority across the organization
B. Authority to implement strategic changes
C. Limited to requesting and negotiating
D. Complete control over the company's finances

96. How can directors demonstrate management success to executives and stakeholders?

A. By expanding their department
B. By using performance metrics
C. By hiring more managers
D. By increasing shareholder dividends

97. In the context of tactical management, what do directors do if they lack the authority to make changes in certain areas?

A. They resign from their positions
B. They follow the strategic plans without question
C. They request and negotiate for what is needed
D. They focus solely on their department without supporting strategic goals

98. Which international control organizations are only open to government membership?

A. COSO, ISO, and OECD
B. COSO, ISACA, and OECD
C. NIST, ISO, and COSO
D. ISO, NIST, and ISACA

99. What does the Capability Maturity Model (CMM) rating scale imply when an organization reaches level 5?

A. The activity is not occurring.
B. The initial activity has been successful.
C. The activity is repeatable but not consistent.
D. The activity is statistically controlled for continuous improvement.

100. What is the primary purpose of implementing IT governance controls according to the text?

A. To ensure that management can avoid any form of risk.
B. To guarantee that the organization will not suffer any data breaches.
C. To ensure that risks are properly managed by mitigation, avoidance, or transfer.
D. To comply with the mandatory requirements of the World Trade Organization.

101. According to the text, which management control method involves aggressive monitoring of user activity?

A. Performance Evaluation
B. Incident Response
C. Active Monitoring (Detective)
D. Human Resources Management

102. Which act mandates strong security controls for data integrity and is mentioned in the text?

A. Foreign Intelligence Surveillance Act
B. Health Insurance Portability and Accountability Act
C. Sarbanes-Oxley Act
D. Federal Information Security Management Act

103. What is the major concern when planning for transborder communication?

A. Ensuring the data is entertaining and engaging.
B. Guaranteeing high-speed internet connectivity.

C. Protecting data security and verifying legal compliance.
D. Maintaining the physical infrastructure of communication lines.

104. What is the purpose of conducting recurring criminal background checks on personnel in regulated industries?

A. To comply with the requirements of the World Trade Organization
B. To fulfill the organization's strategic plan
C. To comply with legal requirements and ensure no unauthorized access
D. To prepare for the annual postimplementation system review

105. What is a key performance indicator (KPI) and what is its limitation?

A. A KPI is a historical average of monitored events and may indicate failing scores too late.
B. A KPI is a forward-looking metric that forecasts future performance accurately.
C. A KPI is a real-time monitoring tool used for immediate performance adjustments.
D. A KPI represents an organization's financial management strategy.

106. What is the result of the following risk management formula: Single loss expectancy (SLE) × annual rate of occurrence (ARO)?

A. Capability Maturity Model (CMM) rating
B. Single loss expectancy (SLE)
C. Annual loss expectancy (ALE)
D. Total risk assessment (TRA)

107. Which model is used by the National Institute of Standards and Technology (NIST) for IT management standards?

A. International Organization for Standardization (ISO)
B. Capability Maturity Model (CMM)
C. Committee of Sponsoring Organizations (COSO)
D. Control Objectives for Information and Related Technologies (COBIT)

108. What is the primary goal of Business Process Reengineering (BPR)?

A. To increase the number of employees in an organization.

B. To document all processes within the organization.

C. To change the way the business operates strategically.

D. To maintain current business processes without changes.

109. Why is it important for an IS auditor to maintain independence during a BPR project?

A. To avoid legal implications.

B. To participate in both audit and BPR team roles.

C. To ensure unbiased auditing of the process changes.

D. To avoid collaboration with other auditors.

110. Which area is NOT a focus for improvement in Business Process Reengineering?

A. Business Efficiency.

B. Improved Techniques.

C. New Requirements.

D. Increasing the number of inspections.

111. When is it common to have two sets of auditors during BPR projects?

A. When the project is too complex for one set of auditors.

B. When there is a conflict of interest.

C. When one set works on the BPR team and another performs verification audits.

D. When the organization is too large.

112. What are the three major areas for improvement identified in BPR?

A. Cost reduction, employee satisfaction, and customer service.

B. Efficiency, techniques, and compliance with new requirements.

C. Marketing, sales, and finance.

D. Supply chain management, human resources, and IT infrastructure.

113. What does BPR often couple with to enhance its effectiveness?

A. Total Quality Management.

B. Continuous Improvement Programs.

C. Enterprise Resource Planning (ERP) implementations.

D. Customer Relationship Management (CRM) systems.

114. What is the key responsibility of management in the context of BPR and internal control frameworks?

A. To solely focus on increasing revenue.

B. To avoid any changes to business processes.

C. To safeguard all assets belonging to the organization and to increase revenue.

D. To document all internal processes without exception.

115. According to the text, which approach is suggested for practical application in BPR projects?

A. Think Big.

B. Incremental.

C. Hybrid Approach.

D. Outsourcing.

116. Which of these is NOT a recommended technique for Business Process Reengineering according to ISACA?

A. Eliminating superfluous processes.

B. Standardizing products across the organization.

C. Automating manual processes.

D. Increasing the complexity of a process.

117. What is an expected result of successful BPR according to the provided text?

A. A decrease in revenue.

B. Comprehensive changes affecting various aspects of the organization.

C. An increase in the number of employees.

D. Standardization of customer preferences.

118. What is the primary objective of operations management in IT?

A. To increase profits

B. To promote consistency with an effective response to user requests

C. To implement new technologies

D. To reduce the number of employees

119. Which of the following is NOT one of the five areas of interest for sustaining operations?

A. Effective leadership

B. Adequate staffing

C. High-risk investments

D. Written procedures

120. What is the responsibility of tactical management in performance tracking?

A. To develop metrics based on user needs

B. To provide hands-on user support

C. To train new IT staff members

D. To sign contracts with clients

121. What should an auditor do when reviewing operational performance?

A. Create new IT policies

B. Obtain copies of signed contracts and gauge performance

C. Take over management responsibilities

D. Lead the IT support team

122. What is the focus of change control?

A. To hire competent IT staff

B. To ensure the best possible decision is reached for changes

C. To document all user requests

D. To reduce the number of IT servers

123. When are IT server and network changes usually scheduled according to one employer's policy mentioned in the text?

A. Anytime during working hours

B. Only on Tuesdays and Thursdays in the evening

C. On Sunday

D. During regular business hours

124. Why should internal auditors be involved in change control meetings?

A. To provide technical support

B. Because they are part of the IT team

C. To contribute their visibility and experience

D. To approve budget allocations

125. What should be the alignment concept of IT efforts according to the text?

A. Towards fulfilling all user requests

B. Towards bona fide goals identified in the business strategy

C. Towards reducing operational costs

D. Towards increasing the number of IT projects

126. What marks a failure in performance tracking according to the text?

A. Any change that is made without approval

B. Performance that does not meet user expectations

C. Each performance item that can't be proven as compliant

D. Any metric that is not developed by tactical management

127. What is the auditor's job in the context of operational delivery?

A. To ensure that proper controls are in place and are appropriate to the unique risks

B. To develop new IT strategies

C. To take part in day-to-day user support activities

D. To manage IT staff and allocate tasks

128. What is the primary objective of every audit program?

A. To increase the profitability of the organization

B. To ensure the organization remains in a competitive position

C. To produce dependable evidence using internal auditors to reduce the financial burden of using external auditors

D. To completely eliminate the risk of compliance failures

129. Which of the following is NOT a usual role for a CISA auditor during an audit?

A. To provide reasonable assurance that audit objectives are accomplished
B. To act as a technical expert providing specific knowledge on the audited processes
C. To ensure consistency in the audit process
D. To report the results of the audit and conduct follow-up activities

130. Who typically manages a program within an organization?

A. Junior team members
B. Project managers
C. Executive vice presidents
D. Internal audit group

131. What is the primary difference between a program and a project?

A. Programs are short-term activities, while projects are ongoing.
B. Programs are managed by an executive vice president, while projects are not.
C. Projects are usually managed outside the normal organizational structure, while programs are within.
D. Projects require internal auditors, while programs require external auditors.

132. Which department is NOT typically involved in PCI compliance audits?

A. Sales
B. Finance
C. Human Resources
D. IT

133. What frequency of audit is suggested for ISO 27002 Compliance?

A. Monthly
B. Quarterly

C. Annually

D. Semi-annually

134. What is the role of technical experts in an audit?

A. To assist auditors with specialized knowledge related to the audit
B. To lead the audit team and make final decisions
C. To supervise the auditor and evaluate the results
D. To conduct the audit independently without auditor involvement

135. In what circumstance might you encounter a Joint Audit?

A. When a single auditor is auditing multiple departments
B. When an organization is too small to require separate audits
C. When two or more auditor organizations cooperate to audit a single auditee
D. When an audit is being performed for internal purposes only

136. What type of audits represent a self-declaration of conformity?

A. External Audits
B. Third-Party Audits
C. Joint Audits
D. Internal Audits

137. Which of the following is NOT a function of the audit program manager?

A. Ensuring that audits are conducted according to overall program objectives
B. Maintaining a centralized record management system
C. Providing technical expertise in specific vendor skills
D. Communicating the audit program and objectives to relevant parties

138. What is the primary purpose of an audit charter?

A. To define the company's financial policies
B. To provide the authority to perform an audit
C. To outline the company's annual budget
D. To hire external auditors

139. Who issues the audit charter?

A. The internal auditors
B. The CEO
C. Executive management or the board of directors
D. The audit committee

140. What qualifications are expected of an audit committee member?

A. Must be a current employee of the organization
B. Should have a background in marketing
C. Must be financially literate and have experience in accounting or finance
D. Should hold a law degree

141. What is not a role of the audit committee?

A. To provide advice on internal control strategies
B. To substitute for executives in governing the organization
C. To review and challenge assurances of internal controls
D. To manage audit activities and results

142. How often should the audit committee meet according to the text?

A. Once a year
B. Twice a year
C. Quarterly
D. Monthly

143. What does the Sarbanes–Oxley Act of 2002 require from executives?
A. To ensure all financial statements are published
B. To certify that all internal control weaknesses have been discovered
C. To personally conduct an annual audit
D. To hold monthly meetings with the audit committee

144. What should be included in the audit charter according to the text?

A. The company's hiring practices
B. The auditor's responsibility, authority, and accountability

C. Marketing strategies for the year

D. A list of the company's shareholders

145. Who is responsible for issuing the audit charter?

A. The CFO

B. The CEO

C. The audit committee

D. The board of directors

146. What kind of letter grants authority for an independent external audit?

A. A confirmation letter

B. An engagement letter

C. A recommendation letter

D. A permission letter

147. To whom should the head of the internal audit and the external audit representative have free access?

A. The CFO

B. The CEO

C. The audit committee chairperson

D. The COO

148. What is the primary difference between an engagement letter and an audit charter?

A. An engagement letter is used for internal auditing, whereas an audit charter is for external audits.

B. An engagement letter records the understanding between the audit committee and independent auditors, while an audit charter does not.

C. An engagement letter addresses the independence of the auditor.

D. An audit charter is legally binding, whereas an engagement letter is not.

149. Which of the following should be included in an engagement letter?

A. The auditee's financial statements only.

B. Independence of the auditors and evidence of agreement to terms and conditions.

C. Only the agreed-upon scope with completion dates.

D. A detailed audit plan with step-by-step test procedures.

150. What is the first step in preplanning an audit?

A. Gathering detailed audit requirements.

B. Assessing the audit team's capabilities.

C. Identifying the objective of the audit.

D. Scheduling the audit procedures.

151. When preplanning an audit, which question relates to the Technology Platform?

A. What are the business rules and objectives?

B. How much space is required to accommodate the staff?

C. Will you be switching from Microsoft to Unix servers for cost savings in user licensing?

D. Who are the people we will work with on the client side?

152. Which of the following is not a duty of the auditee?

A. Confirm purpose and scope.

B. Identify specific standards used for the audit.

C. Provide access to information, personnel, locations, and systems relevant to the audit.

D. Cooperate with the gathering of audit evidence.

153. What should an auditor do if significant restrictions are placed on the scope of an audit?

A. Proceed with the audit and try to work around the restrictions.

B. Render has no opinion or no attestation in the audit report.

C. Ignore the restrictions and gather evidence secretly.

D. Increase the scope of the audit to compensate for the restrictions.

154. What does an assessment typically scrutinize?

A. Only the financial aspects of the auditee.

B. The professional skill level of auditors.

C. People and objects to determine value.

D. The accuracy of the auditor's report.

155. Which of the following is a goal of a Control Self-Assessment (CSA)?

A. To replace the need for traditional audits.

B. To empower the staff to take ownership and accountability.

C. To provide external reporting for regulatory licensing.

D. To attest the claims of the auditee as true.

156. What is the purpose of Shewhart's PDCA (Plan-Do-Check-Act) cycle?

A. To guide a repeating cycle of constant improvement for a process or system.

B. To document the auditor's findings and recommendations.

C. To provide a structured approach to risk management.

D. To identify the financial objectives of the auditee.

157. According to the text, what is an auditor expected to report?

A. Predictions about the auditee's future performance.

B. The truth verified through technical testing.

C. Personal opinions about the auditee's practices.

D. Only positive findings to maintain client relationships.

158. What is the primary purpose of performing a risk assessment in an audit process?

A. To collect all conceivable evidence

B. To ensure sufficient evidence will be collected

C. To focus on non-material evidence

D. To generate high assurance of the truth

159. What does 'materiality' refer to in the context of an audit?

A. The total volume of evidence collected

B. Evidence that is insignificant and could not change the outcome

C. Anything that the auditor finds interesting

D. Evidence that is significant and could change the outcome

160. Which type of risk is associated with the possibility of an auditor not detecting what is being sought?

A. Inherent Risks
B. Detection Risks
C. Control Risks
D. Business Risks

161. What are 'Sampling Risks' in an audit?

A. Risks of using automated technology
B. Risks inherent in the business or industry itself
C. Risks that an auditor will falsely accept or erroneously reject an audit sample
D. Risks that a process or procedure will not be performed correctly

162. What are 'Nonsampling Risks'?

A. Risks after mitigation efforts
B. Risks of not applying appropriate procedures
C. Risks inherent in the business
D. Risks of a control failure

163. How does an audit differ from an assessment?

A. Assessments determine the value of what exists, while audits cannot be used for licensing.
B. Audits are less formal than assessments.
C. Audits are conducted by a qualified auditor, assessments are not.
D. Audits are designed to instill a sense of ownership in the staff.

164. What should an audit risk assessment take into account?

A. Only Inherent Risks and Business Risks
B. Only Detection Risks and Control Risks
C. Only Technological Risks and Operational Risks
D. Inherent Risks, Detection Risks, Control Risks, and other types of risks

165. What are 'Control Risks' in the context of an audit?

A. Risks that the auditor will not gather enough evidence
B. Risks that the auditor could lose control and introduce errors
C. Risks associated with the business's financial status
D. Risks related to the use of technology in audits

166. What might trigger the need for alternative audit strategies?

A. A legal deadline violation
B. Normal day-to-day business operations
C. Recent experiences of outages or service interruptions by the auditee
D. The auditor's preference for different strategies

167. What are 'Residual Risks'?

A. Risks that are not significant for the audit
B. Risks that remain after all mitigation and control efforts
C. Risks that are only present in the preplanning phase
D. Risks that are exclusive to technological aspects

168. What is the primary responsibility of auditors when determining whether an audit is possible?

A. Communicating issues to management
B. Reviewing the auditee's organizational structure
C. Gathering evidence
D. Setting priorities and assessing risks

169. What should an audit charter include when dealing with third-party service providers?

A. A provision for the right to audit
B. A copy of the service provider's latest SSAE-16 audit
C. A detailed organizational structure
D. A mitigation strategy for potential risks

170. What can be a consequence of failing to involve a shop steward in plans and activities in a labor union environment?

A. Improved cooperation

B. Increased efficiency

C. An operational risk of union workers walking off the job

D. Enhanced communication

171. According to the text, which of the following is NOT a response strategy to potential risks?

A. Accept

B. Mitigate

C. Transfer

D. Eliminate

172. What is the purpose of an SSAE-16 audit report according to the text?

A. To ensure individual audits on the service provider

B. To provide detailed evidence to the client

C. To eliminate multiple organizations from individually auditing the service provider

D. To transfer liability to the service provider

173. What does the acronym SOC stand for in the context of outsourcing?

A. Service Organization Control

B. Standard Operational Compliance

C. Secure Operational Certification

D. Systematic Organizational Check

174. What is the possible impact of transferring risk to a subcontractor according to the text?

A. The subcontractor owns financial liability

B. Total elimination of financial liability

C. The client retains financial liability and restitution cost

D. Automatic mitigation of the risk

175. What is the key indicator for the feasibility of an audit?

A. The auditor's personal opinion

B. The client's financial status

C. Sufficient information and cooperation from the auditee

D. The level of risk involved

176. Which of the following is NOT one of the steps in the risk analysis process flowchart provided in the text?

A. Identify threats

B. Determine internal capabilities

C. Calculate impact

D. Obtain external certification

177. What should be done if an audit is deemed not ready after assessing certain criteria?

A. Proceed with the audit regardless

B. Investigate alternatives or find another client

C. Force the auditee to cooperate

D. Outsource the audit to another firm

178. What is the primary role of the lead auditor during the audit process?

A. To communicate issues to the client or auditee

B. To perform technical testing and analysis

C. To guide and manage the audit team

D. To conduct surveys and interviews

179. According to the ISO standards, what is the minimum number of complete audits an auditor with experience should have participated in?

A. At least one complete audit

B. At least two complete audits

C. At least three complete audits

D. At least five complete audits

180. Which method of data collection is considered excellent by the

provided text for in-depth analysis of design parameters, implementation flaws, and faults in the selection or design of controls?

A. Surveys
B. Workshops
C. Computer-Assisted Audit Tools (CAAT)
D. Technical Testing and Analysis

181. What are the three types of controls that should be reviewed during the planning process to detect, correct, or prevent problems?

A. Detective, Reactive, and Corrective
B. Administrative, Physical, and Technical
C. Preventive, Detective, and Corrective
D. Pervasive, Detailed, and Application

182. What is a key component of creating a strong internal control according to the text?

A. Having at least one preventive control
B. Implementing multiple layers of detective, preventive, and corrective controls
C. Using only technical methods for implementation
D. Focusing solely on administrative controls

183. What is the purpose of a skills matrix in the context of an audit team?

A. To create a training program for new auditors
B. To assign audit tasks based on technical certification only
C. To ensure that the team has the right qualifications for specific tasks
D. To track the performance metrics of the audit team

184. When can auditors use the work of others during an audit process?

A. Only when the work has been performed by an IS auditor
B. When it does not meet the audit evidence requirement
C. When the provider's independence, competence, and scope of work meet certain conditions
D. Without any need for review or supervision

185. According to the provided text, what is the minimum level of education required for IS auditors?

A. Bachelor's degree
B. Master's degree
C. Secondary-level education
D. Technical-level certification

186. During the audit planning process, what is the significance of the audit scope?

A. It determines the price of the audit.
B. It identifies organizational and functional units and specific processes to be audited.
C. It outlines the technical skills required for the audit team.
D. It is used to select the audit team leader.

187. According to legal definition, what are the two primary types of evidence in audit?

A. Subjective and Objective Evidence
B. Material and Irrelevant Evidence
C. Direct and Indirect Evidence
D. Qualitative and Quantitative Evidence

188. Which sampling technique is based on the auditor's judgment?

A. Statistical Sampling
B. Random Sampling
C. Nonstatistical Sampling
D. Cell Sampling

189. What is the main disadvantage of nonstatistical sampling?

A. It requires mathematical techniques.
B. It is based on random selection.
C. The results are unlikely to represent the actual population.

D. It is used for compliance testing only.

190. What is the purpose of using Computer-Assisted Audit Tools (CAATs) during an audit?

A. To automate the legal discovery process.
B. To conduct employee performance reviews.
C. To execute automated compliance and substantive tests.
D. To eliminate the need for manual evidence collection.

191. Which of the following is NOT a characteristic of good evidence?

A. Material Relevance
B. Evidence Independence
C. Evidence Objectivity
D. Evidence Cost-Effectiveness

192. Which type of sampling uses mathematical techniques to result in quantifiable outcomes?

A. Judgmental Sampling
B. Nonstatistical Sampling
C. Statistical Sampling
D. Haphazard Sampling

193. What does the absence of evidence in an audit imply?

A. A minor oversight that can be disregarded
B. Proof of compliance with the audit objectives
C. The absence of proof
D. Sufficient indirect evidence

194. In an audit, what is the term for the risk of drawing the wrong conclusion from an incorrect sample?

A. Audit Risk
B. Sampling Risk
C. Compliance Risk
D. Inference Risk

195. What does 'Evidence Independence' refer to?

A. The evidence is obtained without any auditor intervention.
B. The evidence is free from any bias or influence from the provider.
C. The evidence can stand on its own without support from other evidence.
D. The evidence is not dependent on the timing of the audit.

196. What is the term for the investigation of electronic records for evidence to be used in the courtroom?

A. Electronic Analysis
B. Digital Forensics
C. Electronic Discovery
D. Computer-Assisted Legal Research

197. What is the main objective of attribute sampling in compliance testing?

A. To determine the dollar value of the subject population
B. To determine whether an attribute is present or absent in the subject sample
C. To calculate an average by group
D. To estimate the total weight of the combined sample

198. Which sampling method is used when the likelihood of evidence existing is low or to detect fraud?

A. Variable Sampling
B. Stop-and-Go Sampling
C. Stratified Mean Estimation
D. Discovery Sampling

199. What does the precision rate indicate in audit sampling?

A. The number of items to be sampled
B. The acceptable margin of error between audit samples and the total subject population
C. The total dollar value of the subject population
D. The weight of the sample being tested

200. What is the purpose of substantive testing in an audit?

A. To check the activation of system audit logs
B. To verify the content and integrity of evidence
C. To determine the maximum deviation from a procedure
D. To verify that user access rights are in place

201. When conducting substantive testing, what does "unstratified mean estimation" help with?

A. Detecting fraud
B. Estimating the total for the whole subject population
C. Testing for policy compliance
D. Grouping subjects based on characteristics

202. In compliance testing, what is a tolerable error rate?

A. The precision rate of sampling
B. The maximum number of errors that can be accepted
C. The percentage of the subject population that has been sampled
D. The weight assigned to each sampled unit

203. What is a key characteristic of stop-and-go sampling?

A. It requires a large sample size.
B. It allows the auditor to stop testing early if few errors are expected.
C. It is used to calculate an average by demographic groups.
D. It involves testing 100% of the population.

204. What does the audit coefficient represent in the context of audit results?

A. The total value of the audited sample
B. The level of confidence about the audit results

C. The acceptable level of risk in the audit

D. The percentage of the population that is error-free

205. What is meant by a "Nonconformity" in the context of audit findings?

A. An area where the auditee has exceeded requirements

B. An area where the auditee meets minimum requirements

C. An identified violation that needs correction

D. An opportunity for the auditee to make improvements

206. Which of the following best describes "Difference Estimation" used in auditing?

A. A method to verify user access rights

B. A technique to detect system defects

C. A method to determine the difference between audited and unaudited claims of value

D. A sampling method used for large sample sizes

207. What is the primary goal when analyzing evidence samples during an audit?

A. To determine the audit's cost-effectiveness

B. To find out if the auditee has a robust control system

C. To determine whether the samples indicate conformity or nonconformity

D. To assess the efficiency of the audit team

208. What are the two main concerns for auditors related to testing evidence?

A. Sufficiency of evidence and accuracy of the audit plan

B. Contradictory evidence and the audit timeline

C. Sufficiency of evidence and contradictory evidence

D. Audit scope and audit team expertise

209. When might an auditee fail to meet compliance or substantive goals?

A. If the audit plan isn't followed correctly

B. If enough evidence cannot be found to prove conformity

C. If the audit team is not sufficiently trained

D. If there is a lack of cooperation from the auditee

210. What should an auditor do upon discovering contradictory evidence?

A. Immediately end the audit

B. Notify the legal counsel first

C. Perform additional quality assurance checks and retest

D. Report the issue as a nonconformity

211. What is management's responsibility in relation to detecting irregularities and illegal acts?

A. To conduct the audit themselves

B. To implement controls to detect such activities

C. To provide all audit evidence

D. To ensure the audit is completed on time

212. What should an IS auditor do if they encounter indicators of irregular or illegal activity?

A. Ignore it if it's outside the audit scope

B. Notify one level of management higher than where the suspected activities may have taken place

C. Contact law enforcement immediately

D. Confront the individual suspected of the illegal activity

213. Which of the following is NOT listed as an example of illegal activity in the text?

A. Fraud

B. Embezzlement

C. Tax evasion

D. Suppression

214. What is the correct course of action for an auditor who finds a major problem outside of the audit scope?

A. Report it as a minor nuisance and continue the audit
B. Report the finding to the lead auditor or engagement manager
C. Extend the audit scope to include the problem
D. Resolve the problem independently

215. What should an auditor do with a minor problem that's outside of the audit scope?

A. Extend the audit to address the problem
B. Ignore the problem and focus on the audit scope
C. Report the discovery to the auditee and continue the audit
D. Terminate the audit immediately

216. Upon discovering material irregularities or illegal acts, to whom should an auditor report if the activities involve a person charged with governance?

A. The immediate supervisor
B. The lead auditor
C. The highest level possible within the organization
D. Law enforcement agencies

217. What is the first step after performing an audit according to the given text?

A. Reporting the findings
B. Conducting a follow-up
C. Preparing a presentation
D. Consulting with a lawyer

218. What should the final audit report include regarding the auditor's opinion?

A. Only unqualified opinions
B. Either a qualified or an unqualified opinion
C. Only positive findings
D. A statement of the auditor's personal beliefs

219. Which of the following frameworks should be consulted for information to be included in the final audit report?

A. COSO
B. SAS
C. ISACA-ITGI
D. All of the above

220. In the context of an external audit, what should the title of the final report include?

A. The word "confidential"
B. The word "independent"
C. The auditor's full name
D. The audit team's credentials

221. What is the main purpose of the closing meeting with the auditee and management?

A. To negotiate the findings
B. To change the audit findings
C. To obtain acceptance and agreement on the findings
D. To gather additional evidence

222. What should an auditor do if they discover that certain auditing procedures were omitted after issuing a report?

A. Disregard the omission
B. Immediately resign from their position
C. Review audit alternatives or potentially cancel and reissue the report
D. Automatically issue a qualified opinion

223. What is the significance of an auditor's signature on the audit report?

A. It is a formality without legal implications
B. It indicates the report is a draft
C. It attests that the report's findings are true and correct
D. It shows that the report was peer-reviewed

224. What should be done before approving and distributing the audit report?

A. Discard the working notes
B. Distribute the final report to the public
C. Distribute a draft of the report to auditee personnel
D. Share the entire report with all company employees

225. What quality control process is considered very important in every audit?

A. Keeping the report confidential
B. Ensuring the report is colorful and graphically appealing
C. Incorporating auditee comments in the final report
D. Getting the report signed by all auditees

226. What should be done with the final report and working notes after the audit is completed?

A. They should be destroyed for confidentiality
B. They must be archived for document retention
C. The notes should be published separately
D. They should be handed over to the auditee

227. According to the audit process, what is the purpose of the closing meeting with management after issuing a report?

A. To discuss the audit findings with the auditee.
B. To obtain a commitment for the recommendations made in the audit.
C. To take ownership of the problems found.
D. To perform additional risk assessments.

228. Who is responsible for correcting deficiencies found in an audit?

A. The auditor.
B. The management of the auditee.
C. The audit charter.
D. The follow-up team.

229. What should an auditor expect from management if deficiencies from a prior audit remain uncorrected?

A. The auditor should correct the deficiency.
B. Management should provide a valid reason for not correcting the

deficiency.

C. Management should be penalized immediately.

D. The auditor should take responsibility for the deficiency.

230. Who should take ownership of the problems found in an audit?

A. The auditor.

B. The auditee.

C. The follow-up team.

D. External stakeholders.

231. What is the auditor's role when subsequent events that pose a material challenge to the final report are discovered?

A. To update the risk assessment accordingly.

B. To ignore these events if the audit is completed.

C. To potentially adjust the final report based on the nature of the event.

D. To take corrective action on behalf of the auditee.

232. What are Type 1 events in the context of an audit?

A. Events that occur during the audit process.

B. Events that occur after the balance sheet date.

C. Events that occur before the balance sheet date.

D. Events that are not relevant to the audit.

233. What are Type 2 events in the context of an audit?

A. Events that the auditor must personally rectify.

B. Events that occurred before the balance sheet date.

C. Events that occurred after the balance sheet date.

D. Events that lead to the creation of new audit tests.

234. What might be the reason for management not correcting a deficiency identified in a prior audit?

A. The auditor did not communicate the deficiency.

B. Organizational changes have made the deficiency irrelevant.

C. Management is always expected to act without exception.

D. The audit charter prohibits such corrections.

235. What would be a violation of an auditor's independence?

A. Conducting a risk assessment.
B. Reporting audit findings.
C. Taking ownership of problems found in the audit.
D. Gathering evidence during the audit.

236. During subsequent audits, what is the auditor expected to check regarding management's commitments?

A. If the commitments have increased the audit fees.
B. If the auditor's recommendations have been implemented.
C. If the audit charter has been updated.
D. If the auditee has taken ownership of the auditor's independence.

237. What is the primary function of the CPU in a computer system?

A. To provide input and output to peripheral devices
B. To serve as the main data storage component
C. To perform mathematical calculations and process data
D. To manage the boot or IPL process

238. In a computer architecture, what does RAM stand for?

A. Random Array of Machines
B. Readily Accessible Memory
C. Random Access Memory
D. Rapid Allocation Module

239. What is the function of cache memory in a computer system?

A. To store user data permanently
B. To buffer between the CPU and RAM for faster processing
C. To control input and output operations
D. To act as the primary data storage

240. Which component is used for the initial startup process when a computer is turned on?

A. CPU
B. BIOS
C. Cache
D. RAM

241. What is the purpose of the system data bus in a computer?

A. To store data permanently
B. To provide power to the components
C. To allow information flow between components
D. To cool down the system

242. What is the main drawback of computers with a single processor when it comes to system security?

A. They cannot connect to the internet
B. They cannot perform time-sharing functions
C. They interrupt security software during system interrupts
D. They have unlimited data storage

243. How do multiprocessor computers address the bottleneck created by processor-intensive activities?

A. By reducing the need for RAM
B. By decreasing the amount of cache
C. By allocating the load across multiple CPUs
D. By using a single data bus

244. What is the name of the process where a CPU supports light processing for several users at once?

A. Pipelining
B. Boot strapping
C. Time-sharing
D. Interrupt masking

245. In a multiprocessor system, what is the role of the first CPU during the boot process?

A. To act as a task processor only
B. To run dedicated monitoring software without interruptions
C. To run system functions for control, input, and output
D. To store data on the hard disk

246. What is interrupt masking in the context of computer processors?

A. A process to cool down the CPU
B. A technique to prevent the CPU from overheating
C. A method to ignore processing requests to ensure high-priority tasks are not interrupted
D. A way to speed up the RAM

247. Which operating system is commonly used on IBM mainframes?

A. Microsoft Windows
B. Unix/Linux
C. IBM's iOS
D. Apple Macintosh OS

248. What is the most common operating system used in Fortune 500 companies for enterprise servers?

A. Microsoft Windows
B. Unix or Linux
C. Apple Macintosh OS
D. IBM's iOS

249. What is the primary role of a File Server?

A. Serves up information through a web browser
B. Converts server domain names into IP addresses
C. Stores raw data and organizes it in tables
D. Stores data files for shared user access

250. Which RAID level is known for full redundancy by total duplication of data?

A. RAID-0
B. RAID-5
C. RAID-1
D. RAID-7

251. What is the purpose of a Domain Name System (DNS) server?

A. To store and manage website content
B. To store raw data for applications
C. To convert server domain names into IP addresses
D. To provide network storage solutions

252. What is the main security shortfall of using a vendor's default OS installation?

A. Too expensive for most users
B. Lack of advanced features
C. Insufficient user-friendliness
D. Incomplete security settings

253. What type of memory is used for fast, non-volatile storage without moving parts?

A. Flash Memory
B. Magnetic Tape
C. Optical CD-ROM
D. Magnetic Hard Disk

254. What is the advantage of mainframe computers over microcomputers?

A. Higher throughput with very large page sizes
B. More suitable for individual use
C. Lower initial purchase cost
D. Portability and ease of use

255. What does RAID stand for in the context of data storage?

A. Random Array of Independent Disks
B. Redundant Array of Inexpensive Disks
C. Reliable Array of Integrated Disks
D. Redundant Array of Independent Disks

256. What was the primary reason for the Open Systems Interconnection (OSI) model not being widely adopted compared to TCP/IP?

A. OSI was too complex to implement.
B. TCP/IP was already established and more widely used.
C. OSI was more expensive for customers.
D. TCP/IP provided better security features.

257. What is the main purpose of using the OSI model in an audit?

A. To facilitate communication between different computer systems.
B. To identify and correct SoD (Separation of Duties) violations.
C. To replace TCP/IP in network communications.
D. To provide a basis for legal contracts in data communications.

258. Which layer of the OSI model is responsible for defining physical requirements like cables and voltages?

A. Application Layer
B. Network Layer
C. Physical Layer
D. Transport Layer

259. What is the significance of a MAC address in the Data-Link Layer of the OSI model?

A. It is used to identify the manufacturer of the network card.
B. It is used for routing data packets between networks.
C. It is used for encryption and decryption of data.

D. It defines the network protocols used for communication.

260. According to the OSI model, how are IP addresses associated with MAC addresses?

A. Through the Presentation Layer.
B. Using the Transport Layer.
C. By the Session Layer.
D. Via the Address Resolution Protocol (ARP).

261. Which layer of the OSI model is responsible for session control between applications?

A. Application Layer
B. Presentation Layer
C. Session Layer
D. Transport Layer

262. What does the Presentation Layer (Layer 6) of the OSI model define?
A. The data format for communication.
B. The physical connections between devices.
C. The routing of data packets.
D. The establishment of network sessions.

263. Which OSI layer's primary function is to solve user problems through work automation?
A. Application Layer
B. Data-Link Layer
C. Network Layer
D. Physical Layer

264. What is the purpose of subnetting in the Network Layer (Layer 3) of the OSI model?
A. To increase the speed of the network.

B. To facilitate physical connections.
C. To create logical groups or segments for easier management and security.
D. To define the types of cables used in the network.

265. What is the result of dividing an IP address space into smaller subnetworks?

A. Decrease in network overhead.
B. Increase in the number of usable IP addresses.
C. Creation of specific addresses for network name and broadcast purposes.
D. Simplification of the network routing protocol.

266. What was the primary method used to connect the first computer networks?

A. Ethernet cables
B. Serial ports
C. Wireless connections
D. Optical fibers

267. What network device was invented to connect multiple computers together on the same segment?

A. Router
B. Switch
C. Hub
D. Bridge

268. What is the function of a layer 2 bridge in networking?

A. To route traffic between different networks
B. To connect two subnets into the same single subnet
C. To wirelessly connect devices
D. To distribute IP addresses

269. How can a network bridge be configured in terms of broadcast traffic?

A. To filter and prioritize traffic
B. To encrypt data packets
C. To allow or filter broadcasts depending on the manufacturer's design
D. To increase the speed of transmission

270. What led to the development of routers in network design?

A. The need for wireless communication
B. Security concerns with bridges
C. Complaints about too much traffic in one giant subnet
D. The requirement for faster data speeds

271. What was the composition of early routers?

A. A dedicated hardware device
B. A computer with two interface cards and routing software
C. A series of interconnected hubs
D. A complex switch configuration

272. What is the basic function of a router in a network?

A. To encrypt data
B. To convert protocols
C. To forward data traffic when necessary and insulate users on other subnets
D. To act as a firewall and security layer

273. Where can the routing function be loaded in modern networks?

A. Onto a router card in the network switch chassis
B. Directly onto the computer's motherboard
C. Within the hub
D. As a standalone application on each computer

274. Which of the following best describes the traditional routers in terms of their physical setup?

A. Integrated into the computer's hardware
B. A dedicated device in their chassis
C. A software program on the server
D. Part of the network interface card

275. What is the primary advantage of using a bus topology in a network?

A. High cable redundancy
B. Built-in fault tolerance
C. Low implementation cost
D. No single point of failure

276. What is a major drawback of a bus topology?

A. High cost of cable
B. Lack of flexibility
C. A break in the cable affects all computers
D. Complex installation

277. Which topology is the most popular in use today for data networks?

A. Bus
B. Star
C. Ring
D. Mesh

278. What is the primary disadvantage of a star topology?

A. Cable redundancy
B. Flexibility
C. High cost due to additional cabling
D. Reduced network speed

279. How does a ring topology provide fault tolerance?

A. By using a single cable for all connections
B. Through a centralized hub or switch
C. With bidirectional traffic that avoids a breakpoint
D. By having no single point of failure

280. Which technology uses a ring topology for fault-tolerant networks?

A. Star networks
B. Token Ring LANs
C. Telephone networks
D. Telecommunications fiber-optic networks

281. What does a full mesh network provide in terms of network design?

A. Lowest cost
B. Maximum redundancy
C. Minimum cable usage
D. Simplest routing criteria

282. When might a partial mesh network be implemented over a full mesh?

A. When there is unlimited funding
B. When only a few critical links need redundancy
C. When maximum redundancy is not necessary
D. When the network size is very small

283. What is referred to as the N -1 design in network design terminology?

A. Bus topology
B. Partial mesh network
C. Full mesh network
D. Star topology

284. How does the star topology help in reducing cabling costs?

A. By using a centralized hub or switch

B. By extending the maximum recommended cable length

C. By shortening the cable distance to each user

D. By eliminating the need for patch panels

285. What is the primary function of a network hub?

A. To direct traffic intelligently based on IP addresses.

B. To create virtual subnets within the network.

C. To amplify and retime electrical signals for transmission.

D. To connect different networks or subnetworks.

286. Which device is necessary to connect different networks or subnetworks?

A. Switch

B. Router

C. Hub

D. Repeater

287. What is a VLAN?

A. A device that boosts signal strength across cables.

B. A wireless transmission method.

C. A virtual subnet that simulates a private network for a group of devices.

D. A cable type used for long-distance runs.

288. What is a network switch's role in a LAN?

A. To amplify and retime signals.

B. To provide short-range wireless connections.

C. To create discrete communication on each port.

D. To boost signal strength across long distances.

289. How can a VLAN be configured on a network switch?

A. By boosting the signal strength for select ports.

B. By associating specific ports, MAC addresses, or policy rules to a VLAN.

C. By using a Wi-Fi transmitter.

D. By amplifying and re-timing the signals.

290. What equipment is used to divide a network into smaller subnetworks?

A. Hub
B. Repeater
C. Router
D. Wi-Fi transmitter

291. What is the purpose of a bridge in a LAN?

A. To create wireless connections.
B. To amplify and retime signals.
C. To connect two separate networks using the same network addressing.
D. To simulate a subnet for target computers.

292. In what scenario might a Wi-Fi transmitter be preferable over wired connections?

A. For connecting networks over the internet.
B. For counting inventory in a warehouse.
C. For connecting devices in different subnets.
D. For boosting signal strength over long cable runs.

293. What is the primary consideration when setting up a network to meet customer requirements?

A. The color and design of the network cables.
B. The brand of network devices used.
C. The customer's intended usage and connections on the network.
D. The aesthetic placement of network devices.

294. What is the function of a repeater in a network?

A. To divide a network into subnets.
B. To amplify the signal strength to overcome cable distance limitations.
C. To convert between different communication protocols.

D. To provide discrete communication on each port.

295. What is the primary function of DNS in a network?

A. To encrypt data packets
B. To assign IP addresses to devices
C. To route data packets between networks
D. To translate domain names into IP addresses

296. What layer of the OSI model does DNS operate on?

A. Layer 2 (Data Link Layer)
B. Layer 3 (Network Layer)
C. Layer 4 (Transport Layer)
D. Layer 7 (Application Layer)

297. Which protocol can automatically configure the IP address and other network settings on a computer?

A. DNS
B. DHCP
C. HTTP
D. FTP

298. At what layer of the OSI model does DHCP operate?

A. Layer 1 (Physical Layer)
B. Layer 2 (Data Link Layer)
C. Layer 3 (Network Layer)
D. Layer 7 (Application Layer)

299. Why is manual IP configuration still preferred for network servers?

A. It is more secure.
B. It is less complex.
C. It allows for easier troubleshooting.
D. It is required by DHCP.

300. What is a potential problem with traditional DNS mentioned in the text?

A. It is too slow.

B. It is very complex to set up.

C. It lacks security.

D. It does not support fully qualified domain names.

301. What is meant by a fully qualified domain name (FQDN)?

A. A temporary domain name

B. A domain name that includes the top-level domain and the country code

C. A domain name that is easy to remember

D. A domain name that includes the hostname and domain name

302. What mechanism is used to overcome the issue of routers not passing DHCP broadcasts?

A. Secure DNS

B. DHCP helper addresses

C. DNS spoofing protection

D. Subnetting

303. What is the Achilles' heel of DHCP as mentioned in the text?

A. The need for manual configuration

B. The reliance on broadcasts

C. The complexity of setting up

D. The inability to work with DNS

304. What is the preferred method to improve DNS security?

A. Implementing Secure DNS (S-DNS)

B. Manual configuration of DNS entries

C. Using only IP addresses instead of domain names

D. Disabling DNS services

305. What is the primary function of a router with a DHCP-helper-address configured?

A. To forward DHCP requests to another subnet

B. To encrypt data packets for secure transmission

C. To convert high-speed telephone ports into lower-speed ports

D. To distribute static IP addresses to devices on the network

306. Which device is used to connect a LAN to a WAN via telephone circuits?

A. Multiplexor

B. Modem

C. Router with WAN port

D. Access server

307. Which technology is considered the foundation of modern switched networks?

A. Integrated Services Digital Network (ISDN)

B. Digital Subscriber Line (DSL)

C. Dense Wavelength Division Multiplexing (DWDM)

D. International Telecommunication Standard X.25 (X.25)

308. What are the two modes of creating a VPN in an IPsec design?

A. Ad-hoc mode and infrastructure mode

B. Shared key and open system

C. Transport mode and tunnel mode

D. Host-to-host and gateway-to-gateway

309. Which of the following is a major disadvantage of the first-generation packet filtering firewall?

A. High cost

B. Inability to block unwanted access

C. Poor logging and granular rules

D. Complexity in setup and management

310. What does the acronym 'DMZ' in network firewall implementation stand for?

A. Dynamic Management Zone

B. Demilitarized Zone

C. Dedicated Maintenance Zone

D. Data Management Zone

311. Which IEEE standard is considered unsafe for wireless LAN equipment due to security flaws?

A. 802.16 WiMAX
B. 802.11i
C. 802.11a/b/g/n
D. 802.1x

312. What is the best practice for deploying Intrusion Detection and Prevention Systems (IDPS) in a network?

A. Use host-based IDPS on servers and network-based IDPS on backbone segments
B. Install network-based IDPS only on external firewalls
C. Deploy host-based IDPS on all workstations and ignore network-based IDPS
D. Use network-based IDPS systems exclusively for monitoring internal traffic

313. Which type of area network is typically used to connect devices within a building?

A. Metropolitan Area Network (MAN)
B. Wide Area Network (WAN)
C. Local Area Network (LAN)
D. Campus Area Network (CAN)

314. What has been a consistent concept in the delivery of software services from the early days of service bureaus to modern SaaS models?

A. The requirement for local servers
B. The use of printed forms for data submission
C. Reliance on a third-party server for data processing
D. The necessity of dial-up lines for connectivity

315. What term was introduced to freshen up the concept of service bureaus?

A. Cloud Computing
B. Bulletin Board Service (BBS)
C. Application Service Provider (ASP)
D. Electronic Data Processing

316. How is the scalability of SaaS typically managed?

A. Through infrastructure investments
B. By hiring full-time employees
C. With additional subscription fees for expansion
D. Via long-term contractual agreements

317. What is the primary advantage of using SaaS for business transactions?

A. It guarantees complete data privacy
B. SaaS reduces the time needed to transfer business ownership
C. It requires significant infrastructure investments
D. SaaS provides full liability for data breaches

318. Which of the following is NOT listed as a disadvantage of using SaaS vendors?

A. High initial cost
B. Loss of control over data
C. Liability exclusions in service agreements
D. Potential high expense as processing volume increases

319. What is the most accurate description of public cloud services?

A. They have specialized contracts with service-level agreements
B. They offer exclusive use of servers and communication equipment
C. They are often free or low cost with shared resources and limited liability for the provider
D. They are designed for professional associations with high service levels

320. Why might clients opt for private cloud services?

A. For cheaper support costs

B. To avoid any kind of data regulation

C. Because of concerns about data confidentiality and regulatory requirements

D. To share resources with other users for cost savings

321. Which cloud service model includes negotiating tangible service levels and is considered a variation of the public cloud?

A. Hybrid Cloud Services

B. Public Cloud Services

C. Private Cloud Services

D. Cooperative Cloud Services

322. What is the primary reason subscribers are held liable for failures when using SaaS or cloud services?

A. Because the Internet is inherently insecure

B. Due to the high costs of data processing

C. Because clients are responsible for their choice to use the vendor

D. Since all data is public on the cloud

323. What is one of the main motivations for using SaaS according to the provided context?

A. To increase the complexity of IT deployments

B. To improve the internal IT department

C. To reduce infrastructure and operating costs

D. To ensure full liability for data breaches

324. What is the most effective method for reducing operating costs in software development according to the given text?

A. Outsourcing work

B. Cutting staff

C. Improving software automation

D. Reducing software quality

325. What term is used in business to describe the willingness to take questionable shortcuts?

A. Risk management
B. Risk appetite
C. Risk aversion
D. Risk assessment

326. In the software life cycle, what happens after the implementation phase?

A. Needs analysis
B. Production use and ongoing maintenance
C. Software design
D. Selection

327. What percentage of a business's functions are related to common clerical office administration tasks?

A. 85%
B. 50%
C. 15%
D. 70%

328. What type of software requires little customization and provides small but useful financial advantages?

A. Custom-written software
B. Open-source software
C. Commercial off-the-shelf software
D. Strategic systems

329. What is the strategic system's impact on an organization?

A. It performs tasks within a few departments.
B. It provides a small return on investment.
C. It fundamentally changes the way the organization conducts business.

D. It simplifies clerical tasks.

330. Which of the following is an example of a strategic system mentioned in the text?

A. Microsoft Office
B. Apache OpenOffice
C. Auction software used by eBay
D. Departmental databases for helpdesk

331. What is the primary difference between a strategic system and a tactical system?

A. A strategic system is for individual use, while a tactical system is for organizational use.
B. A strategic system offers a higher return on investment for the whole organization.
C. A tactical system changes the way the organization conducts business.
D. A strategic system provides support functions aligned to fulfill departmental needs.

332. What should auditors be wary of when assessing software vendor claims?

A. High prices for open-market software
B. Claims of strategic value with obscure results
C. Custom software for clerical tasks
D. The use of commercial off-the-shelf software

333. According to the text, what is the role of an auditor in the context of software development?

A. To implement the software development life cycle
B. To provide training for software use
C. To determine if organizational objectives have been identified and met
D. To develop custom software solutions

334. Which of the following best describes the Capability Maturity Model (CMM) Level 1 - Initial?

A. Processes are well-documented and repeatable.
B. Processes are ad hoc and individualistic.
C. Processes are defined and institutionalized.
D. Processes are optimized and continuously improving.

335. What is the minimum CMM level required to obtain and maintain ISO 9001 quality certification?

A. Level 0
B. Level 1
C. Level 2
D. Level 3

336. At which CMM level does standardization begin to take place between departments?

A. Level 1
B. Level 2
C. Level 3
D. Level 4

337. In the CMM, at what level are processes quantitatively measured?

A. Level 2
B. Level 3
C. Level 4
D. Level 5

338. Which CMM level indicates that the organization is focused on continuous improvement using statistical process control?

A. Level 2
B. Level 3

C. Level 4

D. Level 5

339. How does ISO 15504 (SPICE) differ from the CMM in terms of levels?

A. It uses different terminology but is fundamentally different.

B. It expands the CMM to include more levels.

C. It simplifies the CMM into fewer levels.

D. It uses slightly different terminology for the same levels.

340. What is the main goal of the CMM according to the provided text?

A. To increase decision authority for department managers.

B. To decrease decision authority for executives.

C. To eliminate decision authority from department managers and workers.

D. To maintain decision authority at the middle management level.

341. What does ISO 9001:2015 emphasize in terms of approach?

A. A risk-based approach.

B. An ad-hoc approach.

C. A fully automated approach.

D. A qualitative-only approach.

342. Which ISO standard is designed to ensure that adequate records are created, captured, and managed?

A. ISO 9001

B. ISO 9126

C. ISO 15489

D. ISO 15504

343. What six quality attributes are defined by ISO 9126 for evaluating software products?

A. Functionality, Ease of Use, Reliability, Efficiency, Maintainability, Portability

B. Compatibility, Usability, Security, Performance, Scalability, Accessibility

C. Design, Functionality, Reliability, Performance, Security, Usability

D. Functionality, Reliability, Usability, Efficiency, Maintainability, Security

344. What is the primary purpose of an Executive Steering Committee in the context of software decisions?

A. To provide technical support to IT departments

B. To manage the day-to-day operations of the IT department

C. To provide guidance and ensure IT functions align with business objectives

D. To handle the financial aspects of the IT projects exclusively

345. What are Critical Success Factors (CSFs) in the context of software decision-making?

A. A list of all potential risks associated with a software project

B. Elements that are essential for achieving strategic objectives

C. The total budget allocated for IT spending

D. Technical specifications that software must meet

346. How should the effectiveness of the decisions made by a steering committee be achieved?

A. Through directive orders from higher management

B. By holding irregular meetings without a set agenda

C. By mutual agreement of the committee members

D. Solely based on the preferences of IT personnel

347. How are business needs typically established during the justification planning of an IT project?

A. Exclusively through external market research

B. By interviewing only the IT staff members

C. From both internal and external sources

D. By considering the personal preferences of the CEO

348. What is typically included in a Request for Proposal (RFP)?

A. Only the financial budget for the IT project

B. A list of current employees and their qualifications

C. An overview of objectives, background information, and detailed requirements

D. An invitation to a company event

349. What is the main advantage of using the Scenario Approach in planning?

A. It helps in creating a detailed budget plan

B. It allows for the discovery of outdated planning assumptions

C. It simplifies the software development process

D. It guarantees a successful outcome for the project

350. What is the role of an IS auditor in the software decision-making process?

A. To write the actual software code

B. To ensure alignment of the system with business requirements and internal controls

C. To make the final decision on which software to purchase

D. To provide ongoing technical support after software implementation

351. What is a key consideration when determining the feasibility of a project?

A. Color scheme of the software interface

B. Availability of right resources to implement the proposed system

C. Number of employees in the IT department

D. The personal preference of the software developer

352. When contemplating software options, what should the organization consider regarding customization and available software?

A. If commercial software is available and the level of customization required

B. The brand of computers currently used in the organization

C. The color preference for the software interface by the employees

D. The number of software developers available in the market

353. What is the main concern with vendors when reviewing proposals for software acquisition?

A. The color and design of the vendor's brochure

B. The vendor's ability to provide low-cost solutions only

C. The possibility of vendors underbidding and overcharging through change orders

D. The personal relationships between vendors and steering committee members

354. What is the primary role of the Change Control Board (CCB)?

A. To preside over IT meetings

B. To authorize and review all change requests

C. To directly implement software changes

D. To manage the company's financial assets

355. Who typically presides as the chairperson of the Change Control Board?

A. A quality control specialist

B. A vice president, director, or senior manager

C. An internal auditor

D. An IT manager

356. What aspect must be included in the change control review process?

A. Input from business users

B. Sole decision-making by IT managers

C. Consideration of the company's financial investments

D. Approval from external consultants

357. When evaluating a change request, what factors should be considered?

A. Business need, required scope, level of risk, and failure prevention preparations

B. Personal interests of the board members

C. Current stock market trends

D. Competitor's business strategies

358. How can one determine if the change management process properly enforces separation of duties?

A. By the number of changes approved

B. By the outcomes of the changes

C. By referring to the client organization's policies

D. By the speed of the change process

359. What should be included in every meeting of the Change Control Board?

A. A group photo

B. A complete tracking of current activities and minutes

C. A celebration of recent successes

D. A brainstorming session for new ideas

360. What is the ultimate goal of the Change Control Board in managing changes?

A. To increase the company's revenue

B. To prevent business interruption

C. To implement as many changes as possible

D. To satisfy individual business unit demands

361. What principles are followed to prevent business interruption during the change management process?

A. Version control, configuration management, and testing

B. Rapid deployment, immediate rollback, and user satisfaction

C. Financial planning, cost-cutting, and investment

D. Outsourcing, partnership, and mergers

362. What is the nature of the approval process for changes within the CCB?

A. Informal and verbal

B. Formal and documented

C. Arbitrary and inconsistent

D. Spontaneous and unplanned

363. What are the two main viewpoints for managing software development mentioned in the text?

A. Incremental and Spiral

B. Agile and Waterfall

C. Evolutionary and Revolutionary

D. Traditional and Modern

364. What is the primary source of failures in the evolutionary development approach?

A. Coding errors

B. Errors in planning and design

C. Lack of user involvement

D. Insufficient testing

365. How is evolutionary software typically released?

A. In a single complete package

B. After extensive user testing

C. In incremental stages

D. Only after all bugs are fixed

366. Which programming languages are associated with the revolutionary development approach?

A. First-generation languages

B. Third-generation languages

C. Fourth-generation languages (4GL)

D. Object-oriented languages

367. What is one major concern with the revolutionary development approach?

A. It requires too much planning.
B. It fits too well into traditional management techniques.
C. It has an excess of internal controls.
D. It lacks internal controls and may fail to obtain objectives.

368. Which project management advantages are mentioned as being used in evolutionary software development?

A. Precedence Diagramming Method (PDM) and Critical Path Method (CPM)
B. Gantt Charts and Status Reporting
C. Earned Value Management (EVM) and Resource Leveling
D. Risk Management and Change Control

369. Which models are used to illustrate the System Development Life Cycle (SDLC)?

A. Waterfall, V-model, and Iterative
B. Waterfall, Spiral, and Agile Prototyping
C. Agile, Lean, and Kanban
D. Scrum, Extreme Programming, and Feature-Driven Development

370. What does the original waterfall model by W. W. Royce and modified by Barry Boehm include that is typically missing in simplified versions?

A. A single unidirectional flow without iterations
B. Validation testing with backward loops for changes
C. A focus on user interface design
D. Continuous integration and deployment

371. What does the spiral model, presented by Boehm, illustrate regarding the SDLC?

A. It only manages one version of the software from start to finish.
B. It shows a linear progression of software development without iterations.
C. It demonstrates evolutionary versions of the software through repeated cycles.

D. It emphasizes the need for a fully planned design before any coding begins.

372. When is the Agile prototyping model particularly useful?

A. When a detailed plan and design are in place.
B. When the team has extensive experience with similar projects.
C. When tasks are unpredictable, and the best design is unknown.
D. When development needs to adhere to strict timelines.

373. What is the main focus of Phase 1 in the SDLC used by ISACA?

A. System Design
B. Requirements Definition
C. Feasibility Study
D. Implementation

374. During which phase of the SDLC are the Entity-Relationship Diagrams (ERDs) and flowcharts developed?

A. Phase 1: Feasibility Study
B. Phase 2: Requirements Definition
C. Phase 3: System Design
D. Phase 4: Development

375. What is the purpose of the System Design phase (Phase 3) in the SDLC?

A. To determine the strategic benefits of the new system
B. To define the detailed system requirements
C. To plan a solution based on objectives and specifications
D. To implement the new system in a production environment

376. Which phase in the SDLC involves writing the individual lines of program code?

A. Phase 2: Requirements Definition
B. Phase 3: System Design

C. Phase 4: Development

D. Phase 5: Implementation

377. What is the primary objective of Phase 5: Implementation in the SDLC?

A. To perform preliminary risk assessment

B. To define the detailed system requirements

C. To synthesize buy and build decisions into one functional system

D. To review the system's effectiveness in fulfilling the original objectives

378. When should Postimplementation reviews occur according to the SDLC?

A. Only immediately after the system goes live

B. Every five years

C. Annually for as long as the system is in production

D. At the discretion of the system owner

379. What is the purpose of Phase 7: Disposal in the SDLC?

A. To define objectives and perform a preliminary risk assessment

B. To plan a solution based on earlier phase objectives

C. To purge data and properly dispose of system equipment

D. To certify and accredit the system for a particular use

380. What does the acronym 'FPA' stand for in the SDLC?

A. Final Product Analysis

B. Function Point Analysis

C. Feasibility Planning Assessment

D. Functional Process Audit

381. Which of the following is NOT a phase in the ISACA SDLC?

A. Product Selection

B. System Accreditation

C. Postimplementation Review

D. Disposal

382. What is the Constructive Cost Model (COCOMO) used for in the SDLC?

A. Defining system requirements
B. Estimating the cost of developing new software applications
C. Implementing the new system in a production environment
D. Disposing of the old system and its components

383. Which of the following is NOT a feature of the ACID model for database integrity?

A. Atomicity
B. Consistency
C. Isolation
D. Flexibility

384. What does the term 'atomicity' refer to in the context of database transactions?

A. Transactions must be of a fixed size.
B. Transactions must be divisible into smaller transactions.
C. Transactions must be "all or nothing."
D. Transactions must be consistent across different databases.

385. In a data-oriented database (DODB), what is used to link tables together?

A. Primary keys
B. Foreign keys
C. Candidate keys
D. Referential links

386. What is the primary advantage of using object-oriented databases (OODB) over data-oriented databases (DODB)?

A. OODB requires a fixed length and format for data.
B. OODB allows for simpler database designs.

C. OODB combines data and program methods into objects.

D. OODB is less flexible and modular.

387. What is the purpose of using the term 'key' in the context of databases?

A. To represent the physical key to the server room

B. To identify a field that is mandatory for every entry in a database

C. To illustrate that information cannot be unlocked without knowing what to use as the key

D. To refer to the graphical representation of a database

388. What is 'referential integrity' in a database?

A. It ensures that data is stored in a single table.

B. It ensures that data is deleted after a transaction.

C. It ensures that data is valid across linked entries in different tables.

D. It ensures that data is consistent within a single table.

389. What do database 'attributes' refer to?

A. Database tables

B. Database rows

C. Database columns

D. Database objects

390. What is a 'tuple' in the context of databases?

A. A unique identifier for a database entry

B. A type of database relationship

C. A row in a database table

D. A type of database key

391. In a database, what is the result of a transaction being 'committed'?

A. The transaction is permanently recorded in the master file.

B. The transaction is backed out of the database.

C. The transaction is stored in a before-image journal.

D. The transaction is divided into smaller transactions.

392. Within a data-oriented structured database (DOSD), what process is referred to when standardizing and removing duplicates?

A. Normalization
B. Atomicity
C. Referential Integrity
D. Isolation

393. What is the primary function of a Decision Support System (DSS)?

A. To automate all business decisions
B. To predict future market trends
C. To render timely information to aid in decision-making
D. To replace human managers with artificial intelligence

394. What is the process of drilling down through data to find correlations in a DSS known as?

A. Data Analysis
B. Data Mining
C. Data Extraction
D. Data Sorting

395. What is the purpose of a data warehouse in the context of a DSS?

A. To act as a primary database for user transactions
B. To combine data from different systems
C. To store backup data
D. To host the DSS software

396. What is a data mart in a decision support system?

A. A tool for real-time data analytics
B. A repository of results from data mining
C. The primary database for storing all organizational data
D. A security feature to protect data integrity

397. What is the typical interface used by a DSS to present information to the user?

A. Command-Line Interface (CLI)
B. Audio Interface
C. Graphical User Interface (GUI)
D. Virtual Reality Interface (VRI)

398. What type of logic might heuristic program rules in a DSS be based on?

A. Binary Logic
B. Fuzzy Logic
C. Quantum Logic
D. Classical Logic

399. Who benefits most from the information presented from a data mart in a DSS?

A. Data scientists
B. Entry-level employees
C. Senior executives
D. IT support staff

400. Which technology represents the next step up from decision support systems?

A. Cloud Computing
B. Quantum Computing
C. Artificial Intelligence (AI)
D. Virtual Reality (VR)

401. What is an open system architecture in computer programs?

A. A system with entirely hidden program logic
B. A system that uses proprietary methods only
C. A system based on well-known standards allowing flexibility

D. A system that prevents data sharing with other programs

402. What is the primary advantage of open architecture?

A. Vendor lock-in
B. Proprietary programming
C. Flexibility and the ability to use best-of-breed programs
D. Encrypted program logic

403. What does a closed system architecture entail?

A. Fully transparent program logic
B. Programs are written without any proprietary methods
C. Methods and proprietary programming owned by the software creator
D. Complete dependence on multiple vendors

404. How do most commercial software products manage data sharing?

A. By preventing any form of data sharing
B. By using an entirely open architecture
C. By being closed systems with open architecture interfaces
D. By storing all data in un-normalized separate databases

405. What is one advantage of closed system architecture for vendors?

A. Flexibility to integrate with multiple sources
B. Locking in customers to their product
C. Open standards and definitions
D. Encouraging customer independence

406. What is a disadvantage for customers using closed system architecture software?

A. Ability to update software easily
B. Ability to use best-of-breed programs
C. Being locked into the vendor's product
D. Reduced flexibility in program usage

407. What is a data warehouse in the context of a DSS (Decision Support System)?

A. A database with real-time data updates
B. A storage for data snapshots with separate un-normalized databases
C. A method for locking in customers to a product
D. A proprietary programming method

408. What is a data mart?

A. A real-time data processing system
B. A subset of a data warehouse designed for specific users
C. A type of open architecture
D. A form of closed system architecture

409. What does 'cleaning and mining' refer to in the context of data warehouses?

A. Locking data to prevent unauthorized access
B. The process of removing redundancies and researching correlations
C. The act of encrypting data within a closed system
D. The interface that allows for data sharing between programs

410. What is one of the main challenges an organization faces in terms of database management?

A. Choosing between public and private cloud services.
B. Determining the color scheme of the user interface.
C. Deciding between a centralized database or a distributed database application.
D. Selecting which office suite to use.

411. What is the benefit of a centralized database system?

A. Higher implementation costs.
B. More flexibility.
C. Easier to manage.
D. Increased redundancy.

412. What is a benefit of a distributed database system?

A. Lower implementation costs.
B. Simplified management.
C. More flexibility and redundancy.
D. Fewer support decisions.

413. Which database system typically carries higher implementation and support costs?

A. Centralized database system.
B. Distributed database system.
C. Both carry the same costs.
D. Neither; costs are negligible.

414. How do centralized systems facilitate mandatory access controls (MACs)?

A. By increasing local decisions on access.
B. By eliminating local decisions on who or what can access the data.
C. By decentralizing data storage.
D. By reducing the number of support decisions.

415. How might decentralized systems impact security?

A. By reducing the number of support decisions.
B. By making it easier to manage.
C. By increasing the likelihood of a security failure.
D. By decreasing flexibility.

416. At which phase in the SDLC would the decision between centralization and decentralization typically be addressed?

A. Phase 1 - Planning
B. Phase 2 - Requirements Definition
C. Phase 3 - Design
D. Phase 4 - Implementation

417. What aspect of electronic commerce might influence the decision between a centralized and a distributed database system?

A. The color preference of the website.
B. The type of products being sold.
C. The requirements for electronic commerce.
D. The personal preferences of the CEO.

418. Which of the following is less likely to be a feature of decentralized systems?

A. Higher flexibility.
B. Increased redundancy.
C. Simplified management.
D. More complex support decisions.

419. What does the increased number of support decisions in decentralized systems imply for an organization?

A. Lower overall costs.
B. Reduced chances of security breaches.
C. Enhanced ease of use.
D. Greater administrative complexity.

420. What does e-commerce stand for?

A. Electronic Commerce
B. Economy Commerce
C. Engagement Commerce
D. Essential Commerce

421. Which of the following is NOT a type of e-commerce transaction?

A. Business-to-Business (B2B)
B. Business-to-Government (B2G)
C. Business-to-Consumer (B2C)
D. Consumer-to-Consumer (C2C)

422. What is the focus of Business-to-Business (B2B) transactions?

A. Sales to individual consumers
B. Online administration of employee services
C. Transactions between a business and its vendors
D. Online filing of legal documents

423. Which e-commerce transactions require compliance with federal employment regulations?

A. B2B
B. B2G
C. B2C
D. B2E

424. What kind of regulations govern Business-to-Government (B2G) transactions?

A. Banking regulations
B. Credit authorization laws
C. Privacy regulations
D. Government regulations

425. What is a specific requirement for vendors in Business-to-Government (B2G) transactions in the US?

A. Maintaining profiles in a banking database
B. Registering with the Central Contractor Registration (CCR) system
C. Providing customer support
D. Complying with credit authorization laws

426. In which type of e-commerce transaction is the provision of customer support and product information included?

A. B2B
B. B2E
C. B2C
D. B2G

427. Why do Business-to-Consumer (B2C) applications require additional logging?

A. Because they involve the online filing of legal documents
B. Because the normal paper trail does not exist
C. Because they are governed by federal employment regulations
D. Because they require compliance with government regulations

428. What special security measures are required for processing online payments in B2C transactions?

A. Strong internal controls
B. Registration in the CCR system
C. Compliance with federal laws
D. Maintenance of company profiles

429. Which type of e-commerce transaction includes online administration of job benefits?

A. B2C
B. B2G
C. B2B
D. B2E

430. According to the text, which of the following is NOT a common perception of IT operations within an organization?

A. The IT department is invaluable like facilities management.
B. IT is a cost center rather than a revenue generator.
C. IT faces the same pressures as business units.
D. IT is similar to a plumber or electrician in terms of operational perception.

431. What is the principal reason for the popularity of IT outsourcing, as mentioned in the text?

A. The high cost of IT operations.
B. The operational problems such as slow response times.

C. The lack of intricate knowledge of how each business unit operates.
D. The desire to adopt new technologies more quickly.

432. What is the first common statement about improving IT operations mentioned in the text?

A. Rearrange Priorities.
B. Buy More.
C. Centralize policies.
D. Update job descriptions.

433. What is the third choice that gets closer to the real solution for improving IT operations?

A. Continuously fighting fires.
B. Rearranging priorities.
C. Committing resources to document and measure the current situation.
D. Buying more IT products.

434. What does IT governance deal with according to the text?

A. Executives recognize their responsibility and take control.
B. IT staff being overly concerned with technology.
C. Creating a corporate culture for recognition.
D. Designing the service delivery operation.

435. In the context of IT leadership objectives, what is the first objective mentioned?

A. Provide detailed directions and support.
B. Define IT's mission with simple words and plans.
C. Centralize policies and standards.
D. Change control from IT to business objectives.

436. How is the perception of IT operations suggested to change according to the text?

A. By wearing formal attire instead of blue jeans.

B. By becoming sharp-looking professionals.

C. By isolating IT further from business operations.

D. By focusing on technology as a safe haven.

437. What are external measures of IT operations as defined in the text?

A. They are the technical details the IT staff is interested in.

B. They are the internal IT department's operational metrics.

C. They are the management's view of IT effectiveness.

D. They are the customer's viewpoint of IT effectiveness.

438. What are internal measures of IT operations as defined in the text?

A. They relate to the customer's ease of using technology.

B. They are the internal workings and metrics interesting to IT staff.

C. They represent the pressures faced by business units.

D. They consist of changing IT policies and procedures.

439. What is the ultimate objective of shifting change control, as mentioned in the text?

A. To focus on IT needs exclusively.

B. To prioritize new product implementation.

C. To align with the specific business objectives of users.

D. To centralize all IT policies and standards.

440. What is the primary responsibility of the IT Operations Managers?

A. Writing computer programs to solve problems for users

B. Directing IT staff in software development, help desk, server, and network administration, and information security

C. Maintaining server hardware and software settings

D. Handling data communication between devices on the network

441. What framework provides a comprehensive set of service management processes focused specifically on help desk operations?

A. Capability Maturity Model (CMM)

B. System Development Life Cycle (SDLC)

C. Information Technology Infrastructure Library (ITIL)

D. COBIT

442. Which role is responsible for the creation of the overall system layout based on data compiled by the systems analyst?

A. IT Director

B. Systems Architect

C. Systems Programmer

D. Information Security Manager (ISM)

443. What does ITIL's service support function include?

A. Service desk, incident management, problem management

B. Software quality assurance testing

C. Network data communication management

D. Writing programs for operating system behavior changes

444. What is the primary goal of IT Operations Management?

A. To generate revenue for the organization

B. To sustain the business needs of the organization's daily user

C. To rewrite or modify the operating system kernel

D. To maintain control over data and software licenses

445. What is the role of the Information Systems Security Analyst (ISSA)?

A. To manage the server hardware and software

B. To maintain the database systems

C. To work with every department to improve their security posture

D. To write computer programs for users

446. Which of the following best describes lights-out operations?

A. Operations run by a large number of personnel

B. Fully automated or remotely controlled operations with no personnel in

the control room or data center

C. Operations that occur during the daytime only

D. Operations managed by the IT director

447. What is the purpose of a Service-Level Agreement (SLA)?

A. To define the responsibilities of IT Operations Managers

B. To establish a formal contract between a service provider and a user defining performance criteria

C. To outline the duties of the Information Security Manager (ISM)

D. To provide detailed job descriptions for IT department roles

448. What is the purpose of IT asset management?

A. To manage the IT department's budget

B. To control and govern the organization's digital assets

C. To provide support for business methods in technology

D. To write programs that change the behavior of applications

449. Who has the responsibility to ensure that backup media is tracked and safely stored?

A. Help Desk personnel

B. Media Librarian

C. Systems Analyst

D. Database Administrator

450. What is the primary focus of capacity management?

A. Designing new computing resources

B. Monitoring and planning for future availability of computing resources

C. Eliminating all single points of failure

D. Selling cloud services on-demand

451. Which tool is used by IT administrators for estimating system capacity needs?

A. Development tools

B. System-monitoring tools

C. Financial analysis software

D. Project management software

452. What can system utilization reports provide insight into?

A. User satisfaction levels

B. The current processing workload

C. The financial status of the company

D. Security vulnerabilities

453. What can directly impact available capacity?

A. The quality of the system's hardware components

B. Changes in service-level agreements or number of users

C. The brand of the system's hardware components

D. The color of the system's hardware components

454. Why do cloud services often discourage planning for capacity by clients?

A. Because cloud services are unreliable

B. Because cloud services require manual intervention

C. Because cloud services are sold as available on-demand

D. Because cloud services are too complex for clients to understand

455. What is a common inevitability in systems concerning single points of failure?

A. They are impossible to identify

B. They are always eliminated by IT administrators

C. There will always be a few due to technology or cost of redundancy

D. They do not impact system performance

456. How does hardware redundancy via duplicate firewalls affect operating capacity?

A. It has no effect on capacity
B. It reduces capacity by half
C. It doubles available capacity
D. It quadruples available capacity

457. What is the result of sharing the workload between duplicate firewalls?

A. Increased security risk
B. Decreased network reliability
C. Two independent communication paths
D. Slower data processing speeds

458. What is the primary objective of information security management?

A. To ensure the organization's data is shared widely.
B. To ensure confidentiality, integrity, and availability of computing resources.
C. To ensure the physical security of the organization's premises.
D. To ensure that all employees understand the IT governance policies.

459. Who is responsible for defining and enforcing security policies within an organization?

A. Chief Privacy Officer
B. Data User
C. Chief Information Security Officer
D. Information Systems Security Analyst

460. What are the major risks of not having an information classification scheme?

A. Information will be mishandled and all data may be scrutinized during legal proceedings.
B. Increased costs in data storage and management.
C. Simplified data retention and disposal processes.
D. Enhanced data availability for users.

461. What role does a Data Custodian play in information security management?

A. They are responsible for the content of the data.
B. They are responsible for the business use of the data.
C. They implement data storage safeguards and ensure data availability.
D. They oversee the entire IT security governance.

462. What is the purpose of documenting the physical access paths to data?

A. To provide a historical record of data access.
B. To ensure accountability and perform risk assessments.
C. To increase the efficiency of data retrieval.
D. To simplify the network administration.

463. Which position is primarily responsible for protecting the confidential information of clients and employees?

A. Chief Information Security Officer
B. Chief Privacy Officer
C. Data Owner
D. Information Systems Security Manager

464. What is the purpose of the information classification process?

A. To categorize information based on the level of detail it contains.
B. To ensure proper handling of information based on its content and context.
C. To reduce the costs associated with data storage.
D. To increase the accessibility of information to users.

465. What should be the basis for data retention requirements?

A. The personal preferences of the data owner.
B. The value of the data, its useful life, and legal requirements.
C. The size and type of the data files.
D. The technology used for data storage.

466. How are software licenses viewed within an organization?

A. As a minor operational cost.

B. As a regulatory compliance formality.

C. As assets that require control and management.

D. As a flexible guideline for software usage.

467. What is the purpose of compensating controls?

A. To replace all other types of controls.

B. To provide additional security in highly secure areas.

C. To serve as backup for failed technical controls.

D. To achieve equivalent levels of protection when preferred controls cannot be implemented.

468. What is the first phase in the incident response life cycle?

A. Detection and Analysis

B. Containment, Eradication, and Recovery

C. Preparation

D. Post-Incident Activity

469. Which of the following is NOT considered a source for detecting IT incidents?

A. User reports to the help desk

B. System log reports

C. Scheduled IT maintenance reports

D. IT's constant monitoring

470. What is the role of an IS auditor in personnel management?

A. To provide technical support to the IT staff

B. To manage the IT department's budget

C. To determine whether appropriate controls are in place to manage the activities of people

D. To develop training programs for IT staff

471. What is the purpose of problem management in IT operations?

A. To provide technical training to new employees
B. To ensure a timely response to issues using predefined procedures
C. To manage IT projects and development
D. To conduct regular performance appraisals for IT staff

472. What should be triggered by the discovery of an Acceptable Use Policy (AUP) violation?

A. Employee termination
B. The incident-handling process and notification to human resources
C. A formal warning to the employee
D. A public announcement of the violation

473. What may indicate that a computer processing job has ended too fast?

A. An increase in system performance
B. A portion of the processing was skipped
C. Scheduled system maintenance
D. A successful system update

474. What is the role of the Incident Response Team (IRT)?

A. To manage daily IT operations
B. To conduct regular system audits
C. To analyze and respond to security incidents
D. To develop new IT policies and procedures

475. Which strategy is used to save money by reducing the occurrence of problems?

A. Budget cuts in the IT department
B. Implementing preventative controls
C. Outsourcing IT services
D. Increasing staff in the IT department

476. What does the forensic life cycle's acquisition phase deal with?

A. Training forensic analysts
B. Acquiring data from the best possible sources
C. Utilizing forensic data in court
D. Reviewing the effectiveness of forensic tools

477. What is a key requirement before starting a digital forensic investigation?

A. Notifying all employees about the investigation
B. Receiving lawful authorization with a clear, written mandate
C. Upgrading forensic software to the latest version
D. Publicizing the investigation to deter future incidents

478. According to the text, what is the primary goal of system monitoring in IT service delivery?

A. To ensure that the hardware is the latest model
B. To uncover operational inconsistencies, errors, and processing failures
C. To monitor employee activities and productivity
D. To ensure that the organization's website is running smoothly

479. What should be enabled and configured to capture security-related information, such as error conditions and login attempts?

A. Antivirus software
B. Firewalls
C. Event logs and audit logs
D. Intrusion detection systems

480. What does the acronym SCAP stand for, and what is its purpose?

A. Standard Computer Analysis Program - for analyzing computer performance
B. Security Content Automation Protocol - for verifying the security state of the system

C. System Control Access Point - for controlling system access
D. Secure Configurations for Application Platforms - for securing application settings

481. What is the recommended practice for centralized system logging?

A. To disable it for better performance
B. To have logs printed and manually reviewed
C. To have logs forwarded to a centralized console for review
D. To store logs on individual systems only

482. Which one of these is NOT a category of uptime-downtime reporting?

A. Uptime
B. Downtime
C. Scheduled outage for service
D. Partial uptime

483. What constitutes a logical access path for a computer system?

A. Only the physical cable connections to the computer
B. The hardware components within the computer
C. The layers of electronics and software that operate as a combined system
D. The physical keys used to unlock the computer room

484. What is the principle of 'least privilege' as it applies to system access controls?

A. Users should be granted the most privileges possible to ensure system usability
B. Users should be granted only the privileges that are necessary for the completion of their job
C. All users should have the same level of access to simplify management
D. Privileges should be assigned randomly to users

485. What is a critical step to perform before deleting a user's account when they are no longer employed by the organization?

A. Increase their access privileges

B. Archive and forward the user's data files to the appropriate department manager

C. Delete all the user's emails and documents immediately

D. Publicize the user's departure on the company's website

486. What should be done with maintenance login accounts in a production system?

A. They should be left open for ease of use

B. They should be disabled

C. They should have their passwords reset daily

D. They should be shared among all IT staff

487. What is the purpose of application processing controls?

A. To ensure the physical security of the servers

B. To monitor employee behavior and prevent data breaches

C. To ensure system security and integrity through internal processing controls

D. To log user activities for audit purposes

488. What is the primary drawback of using traditional tumbler locks for physical security?

A. They are too expensive to install.

B. They are difficult to operate.

C. They are easy to pick or break.

D. They do not provide an audit trail of who has opened the lock.

489. Closed-circuit television (CCTV) systems in security can provide which of the following benefits?

A. Real-time monitoring

B. Audit logs of past activity

C. Both A and B

D. Neither A nor B

490. What is a significant advantage of cipher locks over traditional locks?

A. They are completely mechanical.
B. They use a unique code for each individual.
C. They are less expensive.
D. They do not require any power source.

491. What type of fire suppression system is commonly used in computer installations due to its avoidance of water hazards?

A. Wet Pipe System
B. Dry Pipe System
C. Gas Chemical System
D. Sprinkler System

492. What is the primary purpose of an Environmental Protection Agency (EPO) switch in a data center?

A. To monitor environmental conditions
B. To manage the air conditioning system
C. To kill power to prevent electrocution during emergencies
D. To control the humidity levels

493. The offsite storage facility for data backups should be:

A. Located within the same building for easy access.
B. Bonded with security measures equivalent to the primary facility.
C. Highly visible for emergency recognition.
D. Used for daily operations to ensure data currency.

494. In structured premise wiring, what is the purpose of a suspended cable tray or routing system?

A. To provide an aesthetic way to hide cables.
B. To protect cables from physical damage and accidental disruption.
C. To make cable installation easier for amateurs.
D. To reduce the cost of cable installation.

495. What is a major risk of disposing of computer hard drives without proper data destruction?

A. The hard drives might be reused without authorization.
B. Data could potentially be recovered from the drives.
C. It is bad for the company's public image.
D. It will lead to a surplus of obsolete technology.

496. Which of the following is NOT a recommended practice for ensuring uninterrupted power supply (UPS) in a data center?

A. Connecting to two different power substations.
B. Using a manual power transfer switch only.
C. Having a standby generator in place.
D. Ensuring the UPS can signal the generator to start automatically.

497. Which of the following is the modern-day equivalent to a secret tunnel used during medieval times for confidential access?

A. Firewall
B. Virtual Private Network (VPN)
C. Intrusion detection system
D. Network management

498. What is the primary control for achieving confidentiality in data security?

A. Intrusion detection systems
B. Firewalls
C. Data classification and separation of duties
D. Network monitoring

499. What does the term 'ethical hacker' refer to?

A. A criminal hacker
B. A computer programmer creating constructive programs
C. An individual authorized to test computer defenses

D. A government spy

500. Which of the following is NOT an example of a passive attack?

A. Eavesdropping
B. Social engineering
C. Host traffic analysis
D. Network analysis

501. What is 'spear phishing'?

A. A phishing attack using fake emails
B. An attack targeting a specific server, user, database, or network device
C. A phishing attack using social media
D. A phishing attack with a broad and random target base

502. According to the text, what is the greatest threat to an organization from within?

A. External hackers
B. Script kiddies
C. Employee betrayal
D. Ethical hackers gone bad

503. Which of the following best represents a 'zero-day attack'?

A. An attack using known viruses
B. An attack that exploits a vulnerability on the same day it is discovered
C. An attack that happens during the day
D. A scripted attack using pre-existing tools

504. What is the primary purpose of internal firewalls within an organization?

A. To manage employee internet usage
B. To provide a local barrier for physical intrusion
C. To block attacks from external and internal sources
D. To monitor employee emails

505. What is a 'logic bomb'?

A. A type of malware that spreads through email
B. A dormant code that activates upon a trigger event
C. A tool for network analysis
D. A program that crashes computer systems

506. What type of access control uses labels to identify data security classification and enforces access based on a set of rules and labels?
A. Discretionary Access Control (DAC)
B. Role-Based Access Control (RBAC)
C. Mandatory Access Control (MAC)
D. Task-Based Access Control (TBAC)

507. Which of the following is NOT a characteristic of Discretionary Access Control (DAC)?
A. Uses labels to determine access
B. Allows a designated individual to decide the level of user access
C. Uses simple permissions like read, write, and execute
D. Highly susceptible to escalation attacks

508. In what type of access control does a user's job role determine their level of access to complete work?
A. Attribute-Based Access Control (ABAC)
B. Role-Based Access Control (RBAC)
C. Mandatory Access Control (MAC)
D. Task-Based Access Control (TBAC)

509. What type of authentication factor is a smart card an example of?
A. Something a person knows
B. Something a person has in possession
C. Something a person is (a physical characteristic)
D. Something a person does (a behavioral characteristic)

510. What is the primary purpose of biometrics in authentication?
A. To use passwords more securely

B. To encrypt user data

C. To authenticate based on unique physical or behavioral characteristics

D. To generate digital signatures

511. Which of the following is NOT a use of encryption?

A. To ensure data integrity

B. To prevent data availability

C. To provide confidentiality

D. To authenticate user identity

512. What does a digital certificate in PKI typically contain?

A. The user's username and password

B. The user's public key and identifying information

C. The user's private key and address

D. The CA's private key

513. What is the function of a Certificate Authority (CA) in PKI?

A. To issue digital certificates

B. To encrypt data with the user's private key

C. To manage the user's passwords

D. To distribute private keys

514. Which of the following is NOT a step in the process of using digital certificates for secure TLS communication?

A. Generating a certificate signing request (CSR)

B. Emailing the CSR to the recipient

C. Installing the CA's intermediate public key

D. Updating the program to use HTTPS, SSL, or TLS

515. What is the goal of digital rights management (DRM)?

A. To enable free sharing of digital content

B. To protect digital content from unauthorized access and distribution

C. To encrypt all forms of digital communication

D. To provide a backup of digital content

516. What is the modern evolution of executive scenario planning according to the text?

A. Risk management
B. Business continuity
C. Strategic forecasting
D. Disaster recovery planning

517. What are the two main options executives have when facing financial pressures?

A. Increase revenue or expand market share
B. Cut costs or hire more staff
C. Increase revenue or cut costs
D. Merge with other companies or downsize

518. What challenge does a 30 percent surge in business present to executives?

A. It presents no significant challenge.
B. It is less challenging than a reduction in capability.
C. It presents a challenge of similar magnitude to a 30 percent reduction in capability.
D. It is easier to manage than maintain current business levels.

519. According to the text, what is Information Technology's (IT) primary goal in a business?

A. To innovate new products
B. To keep records available to the business unit
C. To manage the company's online presence
D. To ensure cybersecurity

520. How did the New Orleans and Las Vegas business economies crash?

A. Due to poor management decisions
B. Because of natural disasters

C. Due to external events impacting the local economy

D. As a result of IT system failures

521. What is the common myth about facilities in business, as mentioned in the text?

A. That they are essential for business success

B. That they do not require any investment

C. That they can prevent business continuity situations

D. That they are irrelevant to customer satisfaction

522. What is more critical than the IT systems in a business, according to the text?

A. The marketing strategies

B. The business unit staff, with their know-how and customer relationships

C. The location of the business

D. The vendor relationships

523. What is Wall Street's reaction when key executives leave a company?

A. They show indifference

B. They advise investors to hold

C. They shout orders at investors to sell

D. They encourage investors to buy more

524. What is an advantage for a business in being able to relocate, as stated in the text?

A. It can avoid paying taxes

B. It can ignore market trends

C. It can take advantage of economic constraints, geographic opportunities, or disaster recovery

D. It can reduce its workforce easily

525. What is the stark realization for many professionals regarding the most important elements to protect in a business?

A. The physical assets and inventory
B. The technology and software used
C. The people with the right knowledge and access to records
D. The company's brand and image

526. What is the primary objective of Business "Revenue" Continuity (BC)?

A. To continue operations without funding
B. To halt all activity when something goes wrong
C. To ensure an uninterrupted stream of revenue or funding
D. To rebuild damaged infrastructure to its previous condition

527. Which discipline focuses on the goal of continuing uninterrupted operations, potentially without funding?

A. Business Continuity (BC)
B. Continuity of Operations (COOP)
C. Emergency Management (EM)
D. Disaster Recovery (DR)

528. What is the main strategy behind Emergency Management (EM)?

A. To continue business operations as usual
B. To generate revenue through e-commerce
C. To halt all activity and evacuate people to save lives
D. To rebuild what was lost after a disaster

529. What is a significant risk to business operations outlined in the context of Continuity of Government (COG)?

A. Business may not restart after a major interruption
B. Government officials can commandeer business resources
C. Revenue streams may be interrupted
D. Utilities might fail

530. Which discipline is most associated with the rebuilding process after a disaster?

A. Continuity of Operations (COOP)
B. Emergency Management (EM)
C. Continuity of Government (COG)
D. Disaster Recovery (DR)

531. Which executive role most likely focuses on scenario forecasts and financial controls?

A. CEO
B. CFO
C. CIO
D. Local government official

532. Who is typically in charge during a country's disaster or state of emergency?

A. Local business leaders
B. Federal government agency
C. International organizations
D. Non-governmental organizations

533. What can happen to businesses and homes during a crisis managed by the federal government?

A. They receive additional funding
B. They can be commandeered by the government
C. They are given immunity from damage
D. They are responsible for aiding the government

534. What is often excluded from insurance policies in the context of government commandeering resources?

A. Damage from natural disasters
B. Compensation for commandeered resources
C. Coverage for rebuilding efforts

D. Medical aid for emergencies

535. What is the main concern of the CIO (Chief Information Officer) according to the given text?
A. Revenue generation
B. Continuity of government
C. Saving lives during emergencies
D. Continuity of operations and protecting business records

536. What was the main focus of disaster recovery (DR) during its early stages in the 1980s?

A. Financial stability
B. Rebuilding
C. Brand preservation
D. Customer retention

537. When was the Disaster Recovery Institute (DRI) founded, and what was its initial objective?

A. 1984, to standardize disaster recovery practices
B. 1988, to provide professional practices for disaster recovery planning
C. 1992, to oversee post-disaster reconstruction
D. 2010, to mitigate the financial impacts of disasters

538. According to the text, what critical element did traditional disaster recovery plans lack?

A. Rebuilding strategies
B. IT systems recovery
C. A steady stream of revenue
D. Emergency management procedures

539. What can cause an organization to cease functioning, as discussed under 'Surviving Financial Challenges'?

A. Only natural disasters

B. Breaching significant contractual commitments

C. Lack of a disaster recovery plan

D. Insufficient advertising efforts

540. What can be the consequence for a business if there is a reduction in profit margin?

A. Increase in stock prices

B. Improvement in brand recognition

C. Transformation into an unprofitable business

D. Expansion into new markets

541. What event forced Frontier Airlines to file for bankruptcy in 2008?

A. A natural disaster

B. An operational failure

C. A credit card processor withholding transactions

D. A decline in the aviation industry

542. According to the discussion on cross-coordination between departments, what is necessary for an organization's survival?

A. Regular employee training

B. Weekly BC planning activities

C. Annual financial audits

D. CEO or COO leadership in BC and DR planning

543. How can long delays in rebuilding after a disaster impact customers and investors?

A. They may lead to increased loyalty

B. They may wait patiently for rebuilding

C. They may lose interest and take their money elsewhere

D. They often offer additional financial support

544. What happened to the Frontier Airlines brand name after its original shutdown?

A. It was retired permanently
B. It became a public domain and was reused for a new airline
C. It was sold to a competitor
D. It was rebranded and used for a different industry

545. What does business continuity planning focus on, in relation to disaster recovery?

A. Rebuilding facilities to their previous state
B. Maintaining the public image and survival of the brand
C. Focusing solely on financial recovery
D. Prioritizing IT system restoration

546. What is the primary objective of a business continuity plan (BCP)?

A. To restore IT operations after a disaster
B. To ensure minimal or no interruption to core business functions
C. To reduce the company's operational expenses
D. To expand the business into new markets

547. What was the outcome for US Airways following its software problem in December 2004?

A. They recovered and continued business as usual
B. They were taken over by America West Airlines
C. They filed for bankruptcy but continued operations
D. They ceased operations permanently

548. Why did the Steak and Ale Restaurant Group decide to close all their corporate-owned stores?

A. Due to a lack of resources to pay workers
B. As a strategic move to start a different brand
C. To focus on franchising instead of owning stores
D. To pay dividends to stockholders with remaining funds

549. What advantage does a good business continuity plan provide in terms of financial terms and client attraction?

A. It guarantees higher profits
B. It attracts better financial terms from investors and more clients
C. It eliminates the need for risk analysis
D. It ensures a monopoly in the market

550. What can be a result of an organization demonstrating the ability to continue operations despite challenges?

A. Decreased market share
B. Loss of customer trust
C. Gain of advantage over competitors
D. Financial instability

551. How did the Bank of Italy respond to the California earthquake of 1906?

A. They temporarily closed all operations
B. They set up temporary operations in a wooden horse cart
C. They merged with another bank to avoid bankruptcy
D. They relocated their headquarters to a different state

552. What is one of the benefits of executing a business continuity plan during a higher-than-normal business volume?

A. It allows the organization to reduce its workforce
B. It ensures resources are available for increased demand
C. It guarantees a reduction in operational costs
D. It helps in downsizing the business effectively

553. How did FedEx and UPS compete for market expansion?

A. By lowering their shipping rates
B. By purchasing retail chains to increase drop-off locations
C. By merging with each other

D. By reducing their service offerings

554. What is the potential use of the documents produced during the business continuity planning process?

A. For settling legal disputes
B. For licensing, expansion, reorganization, or outsourcing operations
C. To serve as a historical record of the company
D. As a mandatory report to government agencies

555. Which of the following best describes business continuity?

A. A strategy for IT data backup and recovery only
B. A plan to generate more revenue after a disaster
C. A plan that includes strategies for dealing with disasters and opportunities for revenue generation
D. A program that is only necessary when a disaster strikes

556. Who typically leads business continuity planning in an organization?

A. Chief Operating Officer (COO) or Program Management Office (PMO)
B. Information Technology Department
C. Human Resources Department
D. Customer Service Representatives

557. Which approach to disaster recovery (DR) is likely to be more successful?

A. Running DR as an ongoing program
B. Running DR as a seldom-performed project
C. Having a document with the right title and words for audit purposes
D. Dealing with DR only when a problem occurs

558. What is the main focus of most governments, US DRI, and the Business Continuity Institute (BCI)?

A. Generating new revenue
B. Emergency management and disaster-related preparation

C. Quality data recovery program based on ISO 9001

D. Customer subscription services and new product rollouts

559. What is essential for the success of a Business Continuity (BC)/Disaster Recovery (DR) plan?

A. Limiting coverage to only the highest-value processes

B. Protecting every aspect of the business

C. Focusing solely on IT infrastructure

D. Increasing the company's product range

560. How can an organization's BC plan integrate with other entities?

A. By adopting a competitive pricing strategy

B. By running BC/DR as a temporary project

C. By integrating with supply-chain plans of business partners, suppliers, clients, and government agencies

D. By focusing solely on internal operations

561. According to the text, what is a sign of proper governance in BC/DR planning?

A. The presence of a written plan

B. Assigning tasks on a rare occasion

C. Monthly practice testing and training

D. Relying on overwhelming money and outside personnel

562. What should auditors pay extra attention to during their review?

A. Tasks that are frequently performed

B. Consistently performed tasks

C. Seldom performed tasks

D. Tasks that are outsourced

563. What is the number one priority in business continuity, according to the text?

130

A. Investor relations

B. The customer and the customer interface

C. Having a detailed written document

D. Following ISO 9001 operating rules

564. What is the primary goal of a business continuity program?

A. To minimize insurance premiums for the business

B. To ensure the organization survives significant disruptions

C. To keep all employees retained at all costs

D. To maintain a constant state of technological advancement

565. In the initial phase of setting up a BC program, what is NOT one of the objectives to secure?

A. A sponsor to pay for the project

B. A charter to grant responsibility and authority

C. A detailed risk assessment report

D. Specific business objectives

566. Which of the following is NOT a component provided by executive management in the first phase of setting up a BC program?

A. Active leadership participation

B. Identification of the first target

C. Allocation of unlimited funding

D. Establishment of a BC leadership council

567. What does the acronym 'CSF' stand for in business continuity planning?

A. Critical System Function

B. Critical Success Factor

C. Continuous Strategy Formulation

D. Comprehensive Security Framework

568. What is the role of the Key Goal Indicator (KGI) in the BC program?

A. To determine whether the goal will be reached according to forecasts
B. To indicate each increment of restoration from no-service to full operation
C. To create metrics based on various sources for lower-level forecasting
D. To intimidate executives with liability if they fail to cooperate

569. During the discovery process of a BC program, what is the BIA most concerned with?

A. Calculating insurance premiums
B. Identifying the company's sequence of steps and timing
C. Developing marketing strategies
D. Performing a SWOT analysis

570. In the context of BC planning, what does the term 'RPO' stand for?

A. Recovery Performance Objective
B. Risk Prevention Objective
C. Recovery Point Objective
D. Risk Priority Order

571. Which of the following is not a type of alternate processing location mentioned in BC planning?

A. Redundant Site
B. Hot Site
C. Cold Site
D. Blue Site

572. What is the maximum time systems can be offline before causing damage to the organization referred to as?

A. Maximum Acceptable Outage (MAO)
B. Recovery Time Objective (RTO)
C. Service Delivery Objective (SDO)
D. Business Impact Analysis (BIA)

573. Which team is responsible for interfacing with governmental agencies during a business continuity incident?

A. Emergency Response Team (ERT)
B. External Agency Team
C. Business Unit Recovery Team
D. Communications and Media Relations Team

574. What is the primary role of an IS auditor with respect to a business continuity/disaster recovery (BC/DR) plan?

A. To design the BC/DR plan
B. To approve the BC/DR plan
C. To evaluate the effectiveness of the BC/DR plan
D. To implement the BC/DR plan

575. What should an IS auditor compare to evaluate the selected strategies for a BC/DR plan?

A. The cost of the strategies to the overall budget
B. The results of the business impact and risk analysis to the strategies
C. The number of strategies to industry benchmarks
D. The strategies to the personal preferences of the management

576. Why time delays are considered detrimental to business continuity plans?

A. They increase the cost of the recovery process
B. They can lead to loss of customer trust
C. They can prevent meeting the recovery time objectives (RTOs)
D. They require additional staff training

577. What is the significance of a 0- to 100-hour timeline document in BC/DR planning?

A. It is required for insurance purposes
B. It outlines the order and priority of recovery processes
C. It is used exclusively for training purposes

D. It serves as a legal document for compliance

578. What is generally proposed to handle work backlogs when processing capability is significantly diminished?

A. Outsourcing the work
B. Hiring temporary staff
C. Using manual methods
D. Ignoring the backlog

579. What does an audit of the vital records inventory indicate?

A. The financial stability of the organization
B. The future success of a recovery
C. The company's annual turnover
D. The skill level of employees

580. How often should BC/DR plans be exercised according to best practices?

A. Once a year
B. Once every five years
C. Regularly
D. Only after significant changes in the organization

581. What should be reviewed to assess the most recent training exercise for a BC/DR plan?

A. The resumes of the staff involved
B. The exercise plan, results, and future schedule
C. The financial investment in the training
D. The opinions of the shareholders

582. What is vital to ensuring realistic Recovery Time Objectives (RTOs) in a BC/DR plan?

A. Having a large budget
B. Having the necessary hardware and skills

C. Having a good relationship with vendors

D. Having an international presence

Answers

1. Answer: D

Explanation: Italy's Parmalat dairy scandal, where executives admitted to a non-existent account claiming to hold 4 billion euros, created ISO 15489 as the new standard for records management globally.

2. Answer: B

Explanation: The accounting fraud at WorldCom, where false financial statements were created, resulted in the formation of the US Sarbanes-Oxley Act to establish stronger internal controls in corporations.

3. Answer: B

Explanation: John M. Cinderey misled auditors, circumvented accounting controls, falsified books, and made false statements to auditors, primarily around the proper recording of loan losses.

4. Answer: C

Explanation: New regulations aim to prevent shortcuts and establish a minimum requirement of control, countering the common effect of reduced profits due to increased regulation.

5. Answer: A

Explanation: The US Sarbanes-Oxley Act is similar to the US government's internal controls specified in the Office of Management and Budget Circular A-123, intended for NYSE publicly traded corporations.

6. Answer: C

Explanation: FISMA is related to the security of government information processing and not specifically to banking regulations

7. Answer: A

Explanation: The PCI Security Standards Council oversees the Data Security Standard which relates to credit processing and is aligned with ISO 27001 ISMS control requirements.

8. Answer: C

Explanation: An IS auditor's role is to verify that assets, threats, and vulnerabilities are properly identified and managed to mitigate risk.

9. Answer: D

Explanation: The text describes three types of data: data content (answers), authentication data (keys allowing entry), and metadata (context, usage, labeling), but does not specifically categorize encrypted data as a separate type.

10. Answer: B

Explanation: All regulations aim to ensure that government offices and business enterprises have evidence of operational integrity and internal controls to protect valuable assets.

11. Answer: B

Explanation: A policy is a high-level document that serves as an executive mandate to identify topics of concern related to particular risks the organization seeks to avoid or prevent. It sets the overall goals and is signed by a person of significant authority.

12. Answer: C

Explanation: The absence of a policy indicates an executive control failure, as policies are the chief mandates that establish important control objectives for the organization's success.

13. Answer: B

Explanation: Standards are documents that define specific control points to ensure uniform implementation in support of a policy. They do not contain the workflow for compliance but provide the measurement control points.

14. Answer: A

Explanation: A Regulatory Standard is a control mandated by government law or agency intended to protect the economy, society, or environment.

15. Answer: D

Explanation: Guidelines offer general directions and advice for situations where risks are deemed acceptable and are not managed within a control framework. They are discretionary because they do not provide complete instructions.

16. Answer: B

Explanation: Procedures are detailed "cookbook" recipes that provide a workflow of specific tasks necessary to achieve minimum compliance with a standard. They are designed to maintain control over the outcome of processes.

17. Answer: B

Explanation: Without written procedures, there is a failure to define how to meet established requirements, which legally can indicate dereliction of duty.

18. Answer: B

Explanation: Policies that receive widespread support are typically issued by individuals at the highest levels of authority within an organization, such as elected officials, agency heads, board members, CEOs, CFOs, COOs, and upper vice-level management.

19. Answer: C

Explanation: Auditors should focus on high-risk activities and seldom-used procedures, as these represent greater consequences in the event of failure. This approach helps in identifying areas that require attention to mitigate risks effectively.

20. Answer: C

Explanation: The primary objective of ISACA's code of ethics is to support the implementation of appropriate policies, standards, and procedures for information systems, ensuring that auditors perform their duties with objectivity, care, and due diligence under professional standards.

21. Answer: C

Explanation: Auditors are required to maintain the privacy and confidentiality of information obtained during their audits, except when legal authorities require disclosure. They must not use the information for personal benefit.

22. Answer: C

Explanation: Failure to comply with the code of professional ethics can lead to an investigation and possible sanctions or disciplinary measures against the CISA.

23. Answer: C

Explanation: Theft of intellectual property is considered unethical behavior, and those found guilty of such actions should forfeit all professional certifications, as they are not considered trustworthy.

24. Answer: A

Explanation: Auditors are expected to undertake only those activities for which they are professionally competent and continually strive to improve their competency.

25. Answer: C

Explanation: If an auditor fails to report violations promptly, they may miss the opportunity for amnesty, which could instead be granted to those who report the violation after them.

26. Answer: C

Explanation: Admitting mistakes is important for maintaining honesty. It allows for the mistake to be addressed and resolved, preventing further complications.

27. Answer: B

Explanation: Auditors contribute to the ongoing education of stakeholders by facilitating the use of control self-assessment (CSA), which helps stakeholders understand their problems.

28. Answer: C

Explanation: An auditor's duty upon discovering a finding is to report the issue and state whether it has been fixed or not, maintaining honesty and transparency.

29. Answer: C

Explanation: The ISACA code of ethics strictly prohibits using information obtained during the audit for personal benefit. Auditors must maintain confidentiality and integrity.

30. Answer: C

Explanation: An audit's primary goal is to determine the truth by systematically inspecting records, analyzing and testing evidence, and rendering an independent opinion about internal controls.

31. Answer: A

Explanation: Internal audits involve auditors within their organization looking to discover evidence of what is occurring inside the organization (self-assessment).

32. Answer: C

Explanation: Independent audits are outside of the customer-supplier influence and are relied on for licensing, certification, or product approval, such as independent consumer reports.

33. Answer: B

Answers

Explanation: Process audits evaluate the process method to determine whether the activities or sequence of activities meet the published requirements.

34. Answer: B

Explanation: ISO 9001 is associated with quality management and is one of the standards that auditors may evaluate during business process audits.

35. Answer: C

Explanation: System audits are concerned with evaluating the management of the system, including its configuration, control environment, and incident response capability.

36. Answer: C

Explanation: Compliance audits are conducted to ensure that an organization is following and adhering to a specific standard or regulation.

37. Answer: A

Explanation: Surveillance audits are routine checkups between the certification and recertification audits to verify that the auditee continues to follow the correct procedures.

38. Answer: C

Explanation: Audits differ from assessments in that they are formal processes performed by qualified independent auditors that must be objective and impartial, whereas assessments are less formal and often more cooperative.

39. Answer: B

Explanation: As an auditor in a fiduciary relationship, one is expected to act for the benefit of another person and place the responsibilities to be fair and honest ahead of personal interests.

40. Answer: D

Explanation: The auditor is the person conducting the audit, while the auditee is the organization or individuals being audited. The text clearly distinguishes these as the two main roles directly involved in an audit process.

41. Answer: D

Explanation: The client is identified as the person or organization with the authority to request the audit, which can include any of the listed options.

42. Answer: B

Explanation: The auditor must remain independent, meaning they should not be professionally, personally, or organizationally related to the subject of the audit, nor should the outcome result in the auditor's financial gain or involve the auditor in design decisions of the subject being audited.

43. Answer: B

Explanation: If an auditor is not independent, it casts a shadow of doubt on the objectivity of the audit findings.

44. Answer: C

Explanation: The auditor must disclose any conflicts to the lead auditor immediately to address the issue of independence and possibly be reassigned to eliminate the conflict.

45. Answer: B

Explanation: Involvement in design decisions or detailed specifications would violate independence and disqualify the auditor from auditing any related work.

46. Answer: C

Explanation: The text provides a slogan that emphasizes the importance of objectivity: "The truth is the truth until you add to it," meaning that an auditor should report findings without bias or alteration.

47. Answer: C

Explanation: An auditor should avoid participating in design decisions, detailed specifications, or remediation during their role as this could compromise their independence and objectivity.

48. Answer: B

Explanation: Providing design advice while engaged as an external auditor would violate several standards governing auditor independence and compromise the auditor's ability to maintain objectivity.

49. Answer: C

Explanation: An auditor is expected to report findings that are fair and objective, as per various auditing standards. This is one of the key responsibilities of an auditor.

50. Answer: C

Explanation: The primary function of SOX is to ensure integrity in public corporations by mandating that management provides full disclosure of potential control weaknesses to the audit committee. This is part of the act's objective to create officer liability and ensure corporate officers are accountable for the accuracy of financial reports.

51. Answer: B

Explanation: The word "shall" in regulations indicates that the statement is a commandment of compliance and is mandatory. Failing to meet a required "shall" objective is a serious concern and often non-negotiable.

52. Answer: C

Explanation: The International Organization for Standardization (ISO) is responsible for determining the measurement of products by attributes, such as converting imperial miles to metric kilometers, weight from pounds to grams, and the number of bushels of corn into metric tons.

53. Answer: C

Explanation: The audit charter documents the scope and purpose of the audit and grants the auditor the responsibility, authority, and accountability to perform the audit according to ISACA standard 1001.

54. Answer: B

Explanation: The Basel Accord Standard III focuses on risk management controls in banking as part of the world banking consortium of the G-10 member countries to safeguard international banking.

55. Answer: B

Explanation: Financial audits' main goal is to ensure that executives are held accountable for the accuracy of financial reports, which involves verifying the security and trustworthiness of the IS environment used for financial reporting.

56. Answer: B

Explanation: Materiality in ISACA's audit standard 1204 refers to using evidence that portrays the most accurate story regarding the absence or effectiveness of controls and potential risks to the organization.

57. Answer: C

Explanation: The GLBA sets maximum service outages at 59 minutes for basic account functions, mandates public disclosure of security breaches, and mandatory verification of continuity plans by quarterly testing.

58. Answer: B

Explanation: Corporate officers are ultimately responsible for ensuring financial integrity in an organization. They are required to attest to the integrity of financials and provide full disclosure of internal controls to the audit committee, as mandated by SOX.

59. Answer: B

Explanation: Current sales are considered the primary indicator of the health of a business by executive management. Executives focus on sales to gauge the company's performance, and in a down economy, restoring revenue becomes a critical concern.

60. Answer: C

Explanation: The concept of least privilege refers to providing only the essential information needed to perform a required task. This helps maintain confidentiality and security controls during an audit.

61. Answer: B

Explanation: To ensure confidentiality, auditors should leave all records in the custody of the client unless criminal activity is suspected, and the client should maintain sole responsibility for the safe retention of the archive.

62. Answer: B

Explanation: There is a legal argument that if the client's lawyer hires the auditor, the communication may be exempt from legal discovery under attorney-client privilege, although this does not protect against the disclosure of fraudulent activities.

63. Answer: C

Explanation: Auditors should always wear professional attire that is a level more formal than the attire of their clients. This helps instill respect and confidence in the professional relationship.

64. Answer: A

Explanation: Good leadership involves allowing team members to make comments and ask questions, sharing plans for success, and taking criticism to foster a cooperative environment.

65. Answer: D

Explanation: An auditor should render a numeric score based on the evidence obtained during the audit. If no evidence is available, a score cannot be formed.

66. Answer: B

Explanation: Individuals in IT supporting roles are primarily concerned with purchasing, installing, and supporting commercial off-the-shelf products, and their solutions often follow a specific vendor's product line.

67. Answer: C

Explanation: The archive of the integrated audit usually needs to be kept for seven years, although this period can vary depending on the type of audit and the regulations identified during audit planning.

68. Answer: B

Explanation: Auditors should never place blame on specific individuals when problems are found, as it could be insulting and counterproductive. Instead, they should stick to the facts and maintain a respectful relationship.

69. Answer: B

Explanation: The CEO is primarily focused on generating revenue for the organization by setting the direction and strategy for the company to follow. Their role includes finding ways to attract buyers and increase the company's profits.

70. Answer: C

Explanation: The Audit and Oversight Committee, comprised of directors outside of the normal business operations, has full authority over all officers and executives and can hire or fire any executive.

71. Answer: C

Explanation: The CIO is subordinate to the CFO, who is primarily responsible for internal control. The CIO's authority may vary, but typically, they report to the CFO.

72. Answer: B

Explanation: In a consulting firm, a Partner is equivalent to a divisional president or vice president in a corporate structure and is responsible for generating revenue.

73. Answer: B

Explanation: The Chief Operating Officer (COO) is dedicated to increasing the revenue generated by the business, acting as a delegate making decisions on behalf of the CEO with assistance from the CFO.

74. Answer: C

Explanation: As company officers, the Vice Presidents, along with other executive roles like CEO, CFO, and COO, are usually liable to government prosecutors.

75. Answer: B

Explanation: An Engagement Manager is responsible for managing the client relationship and overseeing the overall execution of the audit and the audit staff.

76. Answer: C

Explanation: A Systems Analyst/Entry-Level Auditor may move up to an Auditor/Consultant role after completing at least three full audits and undergoing additional training.

77. Answer: C

Explanation: The Chief Financial Officer (CFO) is in charge of controls over capital and other areas, including financial accounting, human resources, and information systems (IS).

78. Answer: B

Explanation: Partners in a consulting firm are responsible for generating revenue and also have the responsibility for the professional development of the staff.

79. Answer: D

Explanation: The text specifies that auditors should verify the strategic alignment between IT and enterprise objectives, the process of monitoring assurance practices for executive management, and the intervention to stop, modify, or fix failures. The implementation of the most advanced technology is not listed as one of the high-level management objectives for auditor verification.

80. Answer: C

Explanation: ISACA defines Corporate governance as ensuring corporate executives' ethical behavior towards shareholders, stakeholders, and the protection of organizational assets to maximize the return on a financial investment.

81. Answer: B

Explanation: An IT steering committee is used to convey the current business requirements from business executives to the IT executive. It helps in steering operations to business requirements and ensuring IT efforts align with specific business needs.

82. Answer: C

Explanation: Claude Hopkins would say that the number one critical success factor for a hamburger business to be successful is finding hungry customers. The success of the business is not primarily about the menu, location, staffing, or secret recipe, but rather about satisfying the demand of hungry customers.

83. Answer: D

Explanation: The Balanced Scorecard (BSC) methodology typically includes four perspectives: Customer, Business Process, Financial, and Growth & Learning. Competitive Analysis is not listed as one of the perspectives in the BSC methodology.

84. Answer: C

Explanation: PRINCE2 Practitioner provides a complete step-by-step organizational process methodology and is not theory-only. It is known for giving practical workflow guidance.

85. Answer: B

Explanation: When the Balanced Scorecard is implemented, it changes the way employees prioritize and report their work. Activities and projects are selected based on the value created under established metrics, which also affects employee evaluation.

86. Answer: C

Explanation: The IT steering committee is the principal mechanism for ensuring IT alignment with organizational objectives. It helps in identifying operating challenges, priorities, and desired technical direction.

87. Answer: C

Explanation: For governance to exist in the context of outsourcing, the company must retain the right to audit the service provider. This ensures that the service provider is fulfilling its obligations and that the services are being performed to the company's standards.

88. Answer: B

Explanation: A Project Management Office (PMO) provides centralized reporting of all projects across the enterprise and supports individual project managers with advanced project-planning software, expertise, historical data, and other resources necessary for successful project management.

89. Answer: B

Explanation: Tactical management is primarily focused on selecting maneuvers or techniques that will yield better results, specifically aiming to manage the return on investment for information systems. The text emphasizes the significance of managing this aspect to improve or maintain performance metrics.

90. Answer: C

Explanation: Performance metrics are established and collected to gauge the efficacy of tactical management, specifically to determine if results are showing improvement or decline when compared to a predetermined baseline.

91. Answer: C

Explanation: Individuals at the tactical level, particularly directors, are responsible for supporting strategic objectives set by top management. They do this by implementing plans and solutions within their authority.

92. Answer: B

Explanation: The majority of planning work done at the director level is tactical. Directors are tasked with fulfilling strategic goals through tactical planning and implementation.

93. Answer: B

Explanation: Strategic plans are handed down from top management to the director level, where directors are expected to fulfill these strategic goals through their tactical management efforts.

94. Answer: B

Explanation: Directors are expected to fulfill the strategic goals by providing solutions within their scope of authority, without the power to make changes in other areas of the organizational structure.

95. Answer: C

Explanation: A director's authority outside their department is limited to requesting and negotiating. They do not have the authority to make changes in other areas of the organizational structure.

96. Answer: B

Explanation: Directors can demonstrate management success to executives and stakeholders by using performance metrics to show improvements or maintain performance against the set baselines.

97. Answer: C

Explanation: When directors lack the authority to make changes in certain areas of the organizational structure, they are limited to requesting and negotiating for the necessary resources or changes needed to support strategic objectives.

98. Answer: A

Explanation: The Committee of Sponsoring Organizations (COSO), International Organization for Standardization (ISO), and Organization for Economic Cooperation and Development (OECD) are international control organizations where only governments can be members. These organizations are responsible for setting controls and standards related to world trade.

99. Answer: D

Explanation: The Capability Maturity Model (CMM) uses a rating scale from 0 to 5. Level 5 indicates that the activity is statistically controlled, and the organization is focused on continuous improvement, which is the highest level of maturity.

100. Answer: C

Explanation: IT governance controls are implemented to ensure that risks to the organization are properly managed. This can include mitigating risks, avoiding them, or transferring them (such as through insurance). The controls are not solely about avoiding risk or preventing data breaches, but managing the risks in a balanced way.

101. Answer: C

Explanation: Active Monitoring (Detective) is a management control method that includes aggressive monitoring of all user activity. It is mentioned as one of the minimum requirements of good management and is crucial for providing evidence of performance to the management.

102. Answer: C

Explanation: The Sarbanes-Oxley Act (SOX) is specifically mentioned in the text as mandating strong security controls to ensure data integrity. This act requires companies to follow strict measures to safeguard their data.

103. Answer: C

Explanation: When planning for transborder communication, the major concern is data security, given that sensitive data may not necessarily be secure when communicated over international borders. Additionally, it's important to ensure that the data is legal or regulated across those borders.

104. Answer: C

Explanation: Recurring criminal background checks are required by law for personnel in regulated industries to ensure that individuals with access privileges do not pose a security risk. These checks safeguard information and prevent unauthorized access to sensitive data.

105. Answer: A

Explanation: A key performance indicator (KPI) tends to represent a historical average of monitored events. The limitation is that a KPI may reveal a failing score too late for the organization to implement a change, similar to how a high-school report card may come too late for a student to improve their grades to graduate.

106. Answer: C

Explanation: The annual loss expectancy (ALE) is calculated by multiplying the single loss expectancy (SLE) by the annual rate of occurrence (ARO). This formula estimates the potential annual loss due to specific risk events.

107. Answer: B

Explanation: The National Institute of Standards and Technology (NIST) uses the Capability Maturity Model (CMM) for evaluating and measuring the maturity of governance processes in organizations. The CMM is mentioned as an excellent technical resource for governance models that implement the CMM.

108. Answer: C

Explanation: The primary goal of Business Process Reengineering is to make comprehensive changes affecting the design structure of management, support roles, information systems, and operating policies for strategic change in the way a business operates.

109. Answer: C

Explanation: An IS auditor must maintain independence to ensure that the audit is unbiased and credible. If an auditor participates in designing systems or processes, they cannot audit their work, as this would compromise their independence.

110. Answer: D

Explanation: BPR is focused on improving business efficiency, refining techniques, and adapting to new requirements, not necessarily increasing the number of inspections. In fact, with increased consistency and proficiency, the number of inspections may be reduced.

111. Answer: C

Explanation: It's common to have two sets of auditors during BPR projects to maintain auditor independence. One set works on the BPR team to steer the project, while auditors from a second firm perform the verification audits.

112. Answer: B

Explanation: BPR includes three major areas for improvement: Business Efficiency, where proficiency of workers increases; Improved Techniques, where new improvements in existing techniques are discovered; and New Requirements, where processes adapt to updated regulations, business needs, or customer requirements.

113. Answer: C

Explanation: BPR is often coupled with an ERP implementation, as this can facilitate the redesign of business processes to become more efficient and effective within the framework of the integrated ERP system.

114. Answer: C

Explanation: All internal control frameworks require that management be held responsible for safeguarding all the assets belonging to their organization, as well as for increasing revenue.

115. Answer: C

Explanation: The most practical application in BPR projects is the Hybrid Approach, which begins with a top-down view of the big-picture strategy, followed by bottom-up research to understand current functionalities and define the processes in use.

116. Answer: D

Explanation: BPR techniques include simplifying processes and improving overall quality, not increasing complexity. BPR aims at eliminating unnecessary steps, standardizing processes, and automating manual processes to increase efficiency.

117. Answer: B

Explanation: Successful BPR is intended to involve comprehensive changes affecting the design structure of management, support roles, information systems, and operating policies, which are necessary to survive the challenges of competition and rising costs.

118. Answer: B

Explanation: Operations management in IT aims to support day-to-day business issues by promoting consistency and providing effective responses to user requests, also known as firefighting or user support.

119. Answer: C

Explanation: The text identifies effective leadership, adequate staffing, written procedures, constant monitoring, and the level of staff integration as key factors for sustaining operations, not high-risk investments.

120. Answer: A

Explanation: Tactical management is tasked with developing metrics that are based on specific user needs to track and report the performance of all operations.

121. Answer: B

Explanation: Auditors need to review operational performance by obtaining copies of signed contracts of the organization's clients and measuring performance on each item listed in those contracts.

122. Answer: B

Explanation: Change control is an organized process aimed at ensuring the best possible decision is made for any changes, considering potential unintended consequences.

123. Answer: B

Explanation: The employer mentioned in the text had a policy that IT server and network changes would occur only on Tuesdays and Thursdays in the evening, allowing for work-acceptance test procedures to be run by competent users from relevant departments.

124. Answer: C

Explanation: Internal auditors should be involved in change control meetings to offer their visibility and experience, which presents a valuable opportunity for the client and ensures that changes comply with the best practices of change management.

125. Answer: B

Explanation: IT efforts should be dedicated to bona fide goals identified in the business strategy, not merely to fulfilling requests, ensuring that all efforts support the overarching strategy of the business.

126. Answer: C

Explanation: A failure in performance tracking is marked by any performance item that cannot be proven as compliant with the signed contracts, regulations, or the compliance matrix.

127. Answer: A

Explanation: The auditor's role in operational delivery is to evaluate whether the organization has provided effective daily support following the IS strategy and to ensure that proper controls are in place, appropriate to the unique risks of each source and location.

128. Answer: C

Explanation: The primary objective of an audit program is to ensure the reliability and accuracy of financial information presented by an organization. This is achieved through the production of dependable evidence.

129. Answer: B

Explanation: While a CISA auditor is expected to have technical expertise, their primary role during an audit is not to act as a technical expert providing specific knowledge on the audited processes. Instead, their main responsibilities include providing reasonable assurance that audit objectives are accomplished, ensuring consistency in the audit process, and reporting audit results while conducting follow-up activities

130. Answer: B

Explanation: Project managers typically manage programs within an organization. A program manager is responsible for overseeing the successful planning, execution, and completion of a specific project or initiative. They coordinate resources, set objectives, track progress, manage risks, and ensure that the project meets its goals within the specified time frame and budget

131. Answer: C

Explanation: The primary difference between a program and a project lies in their scope and management structure:

Project: A project is a temporary endeavor undertaken to create a unique product, service, or result. Projects have specific objectives, a defined timeline, and allocated resources. They are typically managed outside the normal organizational structure, often with a dedicated project manager overseeing the project team.

Program: A program is a collection of related projects and activities that are managed together to achieve strategic objectives. Programs are usually within the normal organizational structure and are overseen by program managers. Programs involve coordination between multiple projects and may have a broader scope and longer duration than individual projects.

132. Answer: A

Explanation: PCI (Payment Card Industry) compliance audits primarily focus on ensuring that organizations handling credit card transactions comply with the security standards set by the Payment Card Industry Data Security Standard (PCI DSS). While various departments within an organization may be involved in different aspects of PCI compliance, such as handling financial transactions (Finance), managing employee data (Human Resources), and securing IT systems (IT), the Sales department typically does not directly handle sensitive payment card information or play a significant role in PCI compliance audits. Therefore, the Sales department is not typically involved in PCI compliance audits

133. Answer: C

Explanation: The frequency of audits for ISO 27002 compliance can vary depending on factors such as the organization's risk management strategy, regulatory requirements, and the complexity of its information security management system (ISMS). However, a common suggestion is to conduct audits annually, making option C, annually, and the most likely choice..

134. Answer: A

Explanation: Technical experts play a crucial role in audits by providing specialized knowledge and expertise related to specific areas being audited. Their role is to assist auditors in understanding complex technical aspects, assessing risks, and evaluating controls effectively. Technical experts may include individuals with deep knowledge in areas such as IT systems, cybersecurity, financial analysis, engineering, or any other relevant field depending on the nature of the audit.

135. Answer: C

Explanation: Joint audits occur when multiple auditor organizations collaborate to audit a single auditee, typically to provide enhanced assurance, expertise, or coverage. This approach is commonly adopted in complex or multinational organizations where a single audit firm may not have the necessary resources, expertise, or jurisdiction to conduct the audit comprehensively. Joint audits can provide more thorough scrutiny, diverse perspectives, and broader coverage of audit areas.

136. Answer: D

Explanation: Internal audits represent a self-declaration of conformity. These audits are conducted by personnel within the organization itself, typically the internal audit function or other designated personnel. Internal audits aim to assess and evaluate the organization's processes, systems, and controls to ensure compliance with internal policies, procedures, and external standards or regulations.

137. Answer: C

Explanation: The role of an audit program manager typically involves overseeing the entire audit program and ensuring that audits are conducted in line with overall program objectives, maintaining a centralized record management system to track audit activities and findings, and communicating the audit program and objectives to relevant parties such as stakeholders, audit teams, and management.

138. Answer: B

Explanation: The primary purpose of an audit charter is to provide the authority to perform an audit. It outlines the responsibility, authority, and accountability of the auditor, as well as management's assertion of responsibility, their objectives, and delegation of authority.

139. Answer: C

Explanation: The audit charter is issued by executive management or the board of directors.

140. Answer: C

Explanation: Audit committee members are expected to be financially literate, with the ability to read and understand financial statements, and have past employment experience in accounting or finance, often holding a certification such as a CPA.

141. Answer: B

Explanation: The audit committee is not meant to substitute for executives who must govern, control, and manage their organization. Its role is to provide advice, review and challenge assurances, and manage audit activities and results.

142. Answer: C

Explanation: The audit committee should meet regularly, at least quarterly or four times a year, to fulfill its requirements.

143. Answer: B

Explanation: The Sarbanes–Oxley Act of 2002 requires executives to certify that all internal control weaknesses have been discovered through fully functional detective controls.

144. Answer: B

Explanation: The audit charter should include the auditor's responsibility, authority, and accountability.

145. Answer: C

Explanation: The audit committee is responsible for issuing the audit charter.

146. Answer: B

Explanation: An engagement letter grants authority for an independent external audit.

147. Answer: C

Explanation: The head of the internal audit and the external audit representative should have free access to the audit committee chairperson to ensure open communication of any concerns.

148. Answer: C

Explanation: The primary difference between an engagement letter and an audit charter is that the engagement letter specifically addresses the auditor's independence, ensuring a clear understanding of the auditor's responsibility to remain unbiased and independent in their assessment.

149. Answer: B

Explanation: An engagement letter should include points from the audit charter, the independence of the auditors, evidence of an agreement to the terms and conditions, and the agreed-upon scope with completion dates.

150. Answer: C

Explanation: The first step in preplanning an audit is to identify the objective of the audit, such as compliance with a particular standard or surveillance auditing to ensure adherence to procedures.

151. Answer: C

Explanation: Questions about the Technology Platform may involve discussions about hardware, software, and technological changes such as switching server types for cost savings.

152. Answer: B

Explanation: Identifying specific standards used for the audit is the duty of the auditor, not the auditee. The auditee is responsible for confirming the purpose and scope, providing access to relevant resources, and cooperating with gathering audit evidence.

153. Answer: B

Explanation: If significant restrictions are placed on the scope of an audit that precludes the ability to collect sufficient evidence, the auditor should render no opinion or no attestation in the audit report.

154. Answer: C

Explanation: Assessments scrutinize people and objects to determine their value based on relevance and fitness of use. They are less formal than traditional audits and are usually more cooperative.

155. Answer: B

Explanation: The auditee uses a Control Self-Assessment (CSA) to benchmark progress and improve their score. It empowers the staff to take ownership and accountability for their work.

156. Answer: A

Explanation: Shewhart's PDCA cycle is used to guide a repeating cycle of constant improvement for a process or system, identifying action items necessary to accomplish vague requirements.

157. Answer: B

Explanation: An auditor is expected to report the truth as verified through technical testing. The purpose of an audit is to help management verify assertions through this process.

158. Answer: B

Explanation: The primary purpose of a risk assessment in an audit is to ensure that sufficient evidence will be collected during the audit to support the findings and opinions. This is essential for the audit to be able to prove or disprove the audit objectives.

159. Answer: D

Explanation: Materiality in an audit refers to evidence that is significant enough that it could change the outcome of the audit. Auditors focus on material evidence that either proves or disproves the specific audit objectives.

160. Answer: B

Explanation: Detection risks are those risks that an auditor will not be able to detect what is being sought. It would be problematic if an auditor reports no negative results when material conditions (faults) actually exist.

161. Answer: C

Explanation: Sampling risks refer to the possibility that an auditor might incorrectly accept or reject evidence within an audit sample, which could lead to incorrect audit conclusions.

162. Answer: B

Explanation: Nonsampling risks are associated with the possibility of an auditor failing to detect a condition because of not applying the appropriate procedure or using procedures inconsistent with the audit objective.

163. Answer: C

Explanation: Audits are formal activities conducted by a qualified auditor and generate a high assurance of the truth. They can be used for licensing and regulatory compliance. In contrast, assessments are less formal and are excellent for instilling a sense of ownership in the staff.

164. Answer: D

Explanation: An audit risk assessment should consider a variety of risks, including Inherent Risks, Detection Risks, Control Risks, Business Risks, Technological Risks, Operational Risks, Residual Risks, and overall Audit Risks.

165. Answer: B

Explanation: Control Risks are the risks that an auditor could lose control during the audit process, potentially introducing errors or failing to correct errors in a timely manner.

166. Answer: C

Explanation: The need for alternative audit strategies may arise if the auditee has recently experienced an outage, service interruption, or unscheduled downtime. It is important to allow the business time to stabilize normal operations before pursuing an audit.

167. Answer: B

Explanation: Residual risks remain even after all efforts to mitigate and control other risks have been performed. These are the risks that are left over and must still be considered as part of the overall risk assessment.

168. Answer: D

Explanation: Good auditors are responsible for setting priorities and assessing the risk of the audit to ensure that the necessary functions can be performed. They must communicate issues to management and the audit committee if they are unable to perform the necessary audit functions.

169. Answer: A

Explanation: The original outsource contract should include a provision for the right to audit along with the service-level agreement.

170. Answer: C

Explanation: In a labor union environment, the shop steward must be involved in all plans and activities, and failure to do so may result in union workers walking off the job.

171. Answer: D

Explanation: The four risk responses mentioned are Accept, Mitigate (Reduce), Transfer, and Avoid. Eliminate is not listed as a risk response strategy in the text.

172. Answer: C

Explanation: The SSAE-16 audit report's purpose is to prevent multiple clients of a service provider from conducting individual audits.

173. Answer: A

Explanation: SOC reports are standard Service Organization Control report formats for service providers.

174. Answer: C

Explanation: When risk is transferred to a subcontractor, the client still owns the financial liability and the cost of restitution.

175. Answer: C

Explanation: A good audit relies on sufficient information and adequate cooperation from the auditee to produce meaningful results.

176. Answer: D

Explanation: The steps listed in the risk analysis process flowchart include identifying threats, determining internal capabilities, and calculating impact, but obtaining external certification is not mentioned.

177. Answer: B

Explanation: If the audit is not ready due to any negative responses to critical questions regarding audit feasibility, the auditor should investigate alternatives or find another client to avoid a potential "train wreck."

178. Answer: C

Explanation: The primary role of the lead auditor is to guide and manage the audit team. While they also communicate issues to the client or auditee, the main responsibility is overseeing the audit process and ensuring that the team performs their tasks appropriately.

179. Answer: C

Explanation: An auditor with experience should have participated in at least three complete audits according to the ISO standards.

180. Answer: D

Explanation: Technical Testing and Analysis is considered an excellent method for in-depth analysis of design parameters, implementation flaws, and faults in the selection or design of controls.

181. Answer: C

Explanation: The three types of controls that should be reviewed are Preventive, Detective, and Corrective.

182. Answer: B

Explanation: Creating a strong internal control involves implementing multiple layers of detective, preventive, and corrective controls.

183. Answer: C

Explanation: The purpose of the skills matrix is to ensure that the team has the right people with the right qualifications working on the right tasks.

184. Answer: C

Explanation: Auditors can use the work of others as long as the provider's independence, competence, and scope of work meet certain conditions.

185. Answer: C

Explanation: IS auditors are required to have at least a secondary-level education, according to the table summarizing minimum qualifications.

186. Answer: B

Explanation: The audit scope identifies organizational and functional units and specific processes to be audited during planning.

187. Answer: C

Explanation: Direct evidence proves the existence of a fact without inference or presumption, such as eyewitness testimony or written documents. Indirect evidence, also known as circumstantial evidence, uses a hypothesis without direct evidence to make a claim, based on a chain of circumstances leading to a claim.

188. Answer: C

Explanation: Nonstatistical sampling is based on the auditor's judgment and is subjective, determining the sample size, the method of generating the sample, and the number of items to be analyzed.

189. Answer: C

Explanation: Nonstatistical sampling is subjective and usually based on elements of risk or materiality, making it unlikely to represent the actual population compared to statistical sampling.

190. Answer: C

Explanation: CAATs are used to perform a variety of automated compliance tests and substantive tests that would be nearly impossible to perform manually.

191. Answer: D

Explanation: While cost-effectiveness may be a consideration in audit planning, the characteristics of good evidence include material relevance, evidence objectivity, and evidence independence.

192. Answer: C

Explanation: Statistical sampling employs mathematical techniques to gain an objective representation of the sample, often presented as a percentage.

193. Answer: C

Explanation: If an auditor is unable to prove points due to the absence of evidence, they receive zero credit for their efforts, as the absence of evidence equates to an absence of proof.

194. Answer: B

Explanation: Sampling risk refers to the possibility of drawing the wrong conclusion from a sample that is not representative of the entire population.

195. Answer: B

Explanation: Evidence independence means that the provider of the evidence should not have any gain or loss by providing it, making it free from bias.

196. Answer: C

Explanation: Electronic discovery, or e-discovery, is the process of investigating electronic records to find evidence that can be used in legal proceedings.

197. Answer: B

Explanation: Attribute sampling is used in compliance testing to determine whether a specified attribute, such as a policy or procedure, is present or absent in the sample being tested.

198. Answer: D

Explanation: Discovery sampling is a 100 percent sampling method used particularly in situations where the likelihood of evidence existing is low or when detecting fraud is a concern, such as in forensic audits.

199. Answer: B

Explanation: The precision rate indicates the acceptable margin of error that the auditor is willing to accept between the audit sample results and the characteristics of the total subject population.

200. Answer: B

Explanation: Substantive testing aims to verify the content and integrity of evidence, which may include verifying account balances, performing physical inventory counts, or executing transactions to verify documentation accuracy.

201. Answer: B

Explanation: Unstratified mean estimation is used to project an estimated total for the entire subject population, without dividing it into smaller groups or strata.

202. Answer: B

Explanation:

A tolerable error rate in compliance testing refers to the maximum allowable number of errors or deviations from the standard or regulatory requirements. It indicates the threshold beyond which the compliance test would fail. So, option B is the most appropriate choice.

203. Answer: B

Explanation: Stop-and-go sampling is useful when few errors are anticipated. It lets the auditor cease testing at the earliest possible moment, thus avoiding excessive effort in sampling.

204. Answer: B

Explanation: The audit coefficient reflects the auditor's level of confidence in the audit results, commonly aiming for a 95 percent or higher confidence level.

205. Answer: C

Explanation: Nonconformity in audit findings refers to a situation where testing indicates a violation that needs to be corrected. Nonconformities can include system defects or missing control capabilities.

206. Answer: C

Explanation: Difference Estimation is an audit sampling technique used to determine the difference between the audited (verified) values and the claims of value that have not been audited. This helps in assessing the accuracy of the unaudited data.

207. Answer: C

Explanation: The primary goal when analyzing evidence samples during an audit is to determine whether the samples indicate conformity (meets requirement) or nonconformity (fails requirement).

208. Answer: C

Explanation: The two main concerns for auditors related to testing evidence are sufficiency of evidence and contradictory evidence.

209. Answer: B

Explanation: An auditee might fail to meet compliance or substantive goals if enough evidence cannot be found to prove conformity.

210. Answer: C

Explanation: Upon discovering contradictory evidence, an auditor should perform additional quality assurance checks and retest to determine the reason for detecting the nonconformity.

211. Answer: B

Explanation: Management's responsibility is to implement the controls and supervision necessary to detect irregularities and potentially illegal acts in their environment.

212. Answer: B

Explanation: An IS auditor should notify one level of management higher than where the suspected activities may have occurred if they encounter irregular or illegal activity indicators.

213. Answer: C

Explanation: Tax evasion is not listed as an example of illegal activity in the provided text; examples given include Fraud, Embezzlement, and Suppression.

214. Answer: B

Explanation: The correct course of action for an auditor who finds a major problem outside of the audit scope is to report the finding to the lead auditor or engagement manager.

215. Answer: C

Explanation: An auditor should report the discovery of a minor problem to the auditee and continue the audit within the original scope.

216. Answer: C

Explanation: Upon discovering material irregularities or illegal acts that involve a person charged with governance, the auditor should report at the highest level possible within the organization.

217. Answer: C

Explanation: The first step after performing an audit is to prepare a presentation to report the findings. This precedes the reporting of findings, conducting a follow-up, and consulting with a lawyer, which might be necessary if omitted procedures affect the audit results.

218. Answer: B

Explanation: The final audit report should state whether the auditor is offering a qualified opinion, which means there are restrictions on the findings, or an unqualified opinion, which has no restrictions because the findings have no reservations.

219. Answer: D

Explanation: The Statement on Auditing Standards (SAS), the Committee of Sponsoring Organizations of the Treadway Commission (COSO) internal controls framework, and the IT Governance Institute (ISACA-ITGI) all publish information that should be included in the final audit report.

220. Answer: B

Explanation: For an external audit, the title of the final report should include the word "independent" to reflect the unbiased and impartial nature of the audit.

221. Answer: C

Explanation: The primary purpose of the closing meeting is to review the findings with the auditee and management to obtain their acceptance and agreement, not to change the findings or gather additional evidence.

222. Answer: C

Explanation: If omitted procedures have a material impact on the audit outcome and cannot be compensated by audit alternatives, the auditor may need to cancel and reissue the report. If the impact is tangible, legal advice might also be sought.

223. Answer: C

Explanation: The auditor's signature on the audit report attests that the report's contents are authentic and genuine.

224. Answer: C

Explanation: Before the final approval and distribution, a draft of the audit report should be shared with the auditee personnel who participated in the audit for their opportunity to agree or disagree with the findings.

225. Answer: C

Explanation: Incorporating comments from auditees in the final report is a very important quality control process, as it allows them to voice any concerns or disagreements.

226. Answer: B

Explanation: After the final report is produced, a final copy of the report and the working notes need to be placed into the audit archive for document retention.

227. Answer: B

Explanation: The purpose of the closing meeting with management after issuing an audit report is to obtain a commitment from management for the recommendations made in the audit. Management is then responsible for acknowledging these recommendations and for designating corrective actions, including estimating dates for these actions.

228. Answer: B

Explanation: The management of the auditee is responsible for correcting deficiencies found in an audit. It is their job to acknowledge the auditor's recommendations and designate corrective actions.

229. Answer: B

Explanation: If deficiencies from a prior audit remain uncorrected, the auditor should expect management to act promptly to correct the deficiency and provide a valid reason for not doing so, such as changes in organizational design or practices that have eliminated the conditions of the prior control's weakness.

230. Answer: B

Explanation: All issues raised in audit findings should be regarded as owned by the auditee. It is the responsibility of their management to fix the problems, and the auditor should never take ownership of these problems as it would violate their independence.

231. Answer: C

Explanation: When subsequent events that pose a material challenge to the final report are discovered, the auditor should be concerned and may need to adjust the final report or include additional disclosures based on the nature of these events.

232. Answer: C

Explanation: Type 1 events refer to those that occurred before the balance sheet date. These events are recognized in accounting standards and can affect the audit findings.

233. Answer: C

Explanation: Type 2 events are those that occurred after the balance sheet date. Depending on the type of audit, these may have implications on the reporting requirements or the audit report content.

234. Answer: B

Explanation: Management might not correct a deficiency identified in a prior audit if changes in the organizational design or practice have rendered the original conditions of the control's weakness irrelevant.

235. Answer: C

Explanation: Taking ownership of problems found in an audit would violate an auditor's independence. Auditors must maintain their independence and ensure that issues raised in the findings are seen as the responsibility of the auditee's management to resolve.

236. Answer: B

Explanation: During subsequent audits, the auditor is expected to check whether management has honored their commitments to fix or remediate deficiencies found in a prior audit. The auditor checks if the recommendations have been implemented as agreed.

237. Answer: C

Explanation: The CPU, or Central Processing Unit, is responsible for performing mathematical calculations with the assistance of an internal arithmetic logic unit, cache, and RAM.

238. Answer: C

Explanation: RAM stands for Random Access Memory and is used by the CPU as a working memory space to help run processes effectively.

239. Answer: B

Explanation: Cache memory is a type of superfast memory used to help the CPU run at maximum speed by buffering between the CPU and the slower RAM.

240. Answer: B

Explanation: The Basic Input/Output System (BIOS) is loaded from data storage along with the operating system during the boot or IPL process when the computer is turned on.

241. Answer: C

Explanation: The system data bus is a string of electrical conductors that allows information to flow to and from the electronic components in a computer.

242. Answer: C

Explanation: Single-processor computers halt security software during each system interrupt to process another task, which can compromise system security.

243. Answer: C

Explanation: Multiprocessor systems deal with the demands of processor-intensive applications by spreading the processing load across multiple CPUs.

244. Answer: C

Explanation: Time-sharing is the process where each user or system process receives a tiny segment of time for processing their request, allowing a single CPU to support multiple users simultaneously with little delay.

245. Answer: C

Explanation: The first CPU in a multiprocessor system, when booted, takes on the responsibility of running system functions, including control, input, and output, and schedules tasks across other CPUs.

246. Answer: C

Explanation: Interrupt masking is a technique that allows a CPU to be programmed to ignore interrupt requests, which is useful for ensuring that high-priority tasks, such as security functions, are not interrupted.

247. Answer: C

Explanation: IBM's iOS, not to be confused with Apple's iOS, is common in the IBM mainframe world. It is designed for these large, general-purpose systems that are capable of handling massive volumes of data.

248. Answer: B

Explanation: The most common operating systems in Fortune 500 for enterprise servers are Unix or Linux, followed by Microsoft Windows for user workstations and Apple Macintosh OS for multimedia and graphical purposes.

249. Answer: D

Explanation: A File Server's main function is to store data files and provide shared access to these files on a network, usually through mounted drives or file shares.

250. Answer: C

Explanation: RAID-1, also known as mirroring, provides full redundancy by maintaining two mirror-image copies of data. It is the most secure RAID level in terms of data protection against a single drive failure.

251. Answer: C

Explanation: The DNS server's primary role is to translate human-friendly domain names into numerical IP addresses that computers use to locate each other on the network.

252. Answer: D

Explanation: A major security shortfall of using the vendor's default OS installation is that it often omits necessary security settings, leaving systems vulnerable to attacks.

253. Answer: A

Explanation: Flash Memory is used in a variety of devices for fast and non-volatile storage without any moving parts, making it ideal for portable electronic devices.

254. Answer: A

Explanation: Mainframe computers are capable of processing massive amounts of data in parallel and have very large page sizes, which allow for higher throughput compared to microcomputers.

255. Answer: D

Explanation: RAID originally stood for Redundant Array of Inexpensive Disks, but is now commonly referred to as Redundant Array of Independent Disks. This technology is used for data storage to provide various levels of performance and redundancy.

256. Answer: C

Explanation: The OSI model was not adopted widely because many customers were not interested in bearing the cost of developing the OSI protocols when TCP/IP was a cheaper alternative.

257. Answer: A

Explanation: The OSI (Open Systems Interconnection) model serves as a conceptual framework for understanding how different networking protocols interact and function within a network environment. It helps in standardizing communication protocols, facilitating interoperability between different computer systems and network devices. Option A best describes the main purpose of using the OSI model in an audit, as it emphasizes its role in enabling communication between various systems.

258. Answer: C

Explanation: The Physical layer (Layer 1) of the OSI model is responsible for the physical requirements in data communication, which includes cables and voltages.

259. Answer: A

Explanation: The MAC address in the Data-Link Layer (Layer 2) is a unique identifier for every network card manufactured and is used for "to" and "from" communications within the same broadcast domain.

260. Answer: D

Explanation: The Address Resolution Protocol (ARP) is used to match IP addresses with their corresponding MAC addresses.

261. Answer: C

Explanation: The Session Layer (Layer 5) of the OSI model is responsible for initiating, maintaining, and terminating communication sessions between applications.

262. Answer: A

Explanation: The Presentation Layer (Layer 6) defines the data structure and format used for communication, ensuring compatibility across different platforms and possibly including encryption.

263. Answer: A

Explanation: The Application Layer (Layer 7) is where computer software executes to solve user problems and perform work automation.

264. Answer: C

Explanation: Subnetting in the Network Layer (Layer 3) is used to divide networks into subnetworks or segments, providing better performance and promoting logical separation of duties for security.

265. Answer: C

Explanation: When an IP address space is divided into smaller subnetworks, some IP addresses are consumed in overhead for creating the subnet, including addresses reserved for the network name and broadcast IP, which cannot be assigned to devices.

266. Answer: B

Explanation: The first computer networks were created by connecting serial ports between two or more computers, using modem software to manage file transfers.

267. Answer: C

Explanation: The hub, or shared media access unit, was created to connect multiple computers on the same segment, which is also referred to as a subnet.

268. Answer: B

Explanation: A layer 2 bridge allows all traffic to pass from one side to the next, connecting two subnets into the same single subnet.

269. Answer: C

Explanation: A bridge can be configured to either allow broadcast across it or filter broadcasts to reduce noise, depending on the bridge manufacturer's design.

270. Answer: C

Explanation: The development of routers was driven by the need to connect separate networks without merging them into a single subnet, due to complaints about too much traffic in large subnets.

271. Answer: B

Explanation: Early routers were essentially computers with two interface cards, with one card connected to each LAN, and a software-routing program that directed traffic.

272. Answer: C

Explanation: The basic function of a router is to determine whether traffic needs to cross to another subnet and to forward it if necessary, while protecting other subnets from unnecessary data transmission noise.

273. Answer: A

Explanation: In modern networks, the routing function can be loaded onto a router card installed in the network switch chassis, integrating routing capabilities into the switch.

274. Answer: B

Explanation: Traditional routers are usually dedicated devices housed in their chassis, separate from other network devices.

275. Answer: C

Explanation: The bus topology presents a relatively inexpensive method for connecting multiple computers, making it cost-effective. The design involves a single coaxial cable that passes through the connector on the back of each computer on the network, tying all the systems together.

276. Answer: C

Explanation: A significant drawback of the bus topology is that a break in the bus cable can interrupt transmission for all the computers attached to that cable, potentially causing a network outage.

277. Answer: B

Explanation: The star topology is the most popular in use today for data networks. In this topology, each computer has a dedicated cable connection running to a network hub or switch, offering flexibility and cable redundancy.

278. Answer: C

Explanation: The primary disadvantage of a star topology is the cost of all the additional cables required to make dedicated connections for each station.

279. Answer: C

Explanation: A ring topology provides fault tolerance by allowing network traffic to be transmitted in either direction on a bidirectional loop, which means that if the ring breaks, traffic can still travel through the ring in the opposite direction, avoiding the breakpoint.

280. Answer: D

Explanation: The telecommunications companies use ring technology in their fiber-optic networks to create a fault-tolerant network by allowing redundant paths necessary for network communication.

281. Answer: B

Explanation: A full mesh network provides the highest possible redundancy by having alternate connections for every major backbone point on the network.

282. Answer: B

Explanation: A partial mesh network might be implemented when the cost of a full mesh network is prohibitive, and therefore, only the most critical links are given redundancy.

283. Answer: C

Explanation: Network designers refer to full mesh networks as the N -1 design, which gives the highest possible redundancy. The 'N' stands for the number of points to be connected, and the '-1' refers to the total number of additional connections necessary to achieve a fully redundant mesh.

284. Answer: C

Explanation: The star topology helps reduce cabling cost by shortening the cable distance needed to reach each user. Every cable is terminated at the wall plate near the user and at a patch panel in the wire closet, ensuring that the maximum recommended cable length is not exceeded.

285. Answer: C

Explanation: A network hub is similar to an electrical junction box and its main function is to amplify and retime the tiny electrical signals to allow data to be shared across each port.

286. Answer: B

Explanation: A router connects separate subnetworks or adapts a connection to different transmission media, making intelligent decisions about routing traffic down particular links.

287. Answer: C

Explanation: A VLAN (Virtual Local Area Network) is a method to divide a network into virtual subnets to create the appearance of private communications for groups of devices within the network.

288. Answer: C

Explanation: A network switch operates at layer 2 and provides an intelligent process for creating discrete communication on each port, similar to the function of a PBX telephone switch.

289. Answer: B

Explanation: VLANs can be configured on network switches using a variety of methods, including specific ports, MAC addresses, or policy rules if the switch hardware supports it.

290. Answer: C

Explanation: Routers can be used to segment a larger network into smaller subnetworks or subnets and provide access across these subnets.

291. Answer: C

Explanation: A bridge, especially an intelligent bridge (layer 2 switch), connects two separate networks by using the same network addressing, effectively joining them into one subnet.

292. Answer: B

Explanation: In scenarios where mobility and flexibility are important, such as counting inventory in a warehouse, a Wi-Fi transmitter can be preferable over wired connections. It allows personnel to move freely within the warehouse without being restricted by cables, enabling efficient inventory management. Options A, C, and D do not specifically relate to scenarios where Wi-Fi might be preferable over wired connections.

293. Answer: C

Explanation: Proper identification of customer requirements in terms of what they intend to connect and how they intend to use the network is crucial for aligning the network to the organizational objectives.

294. Answer: B

Explanation: A repeater is designed to boost the signal strength across a cable, allowing the signal to travel greater distances without degradation.

295. Answer: D

Explanation: DNS stands for Domain Name System and its primary function is to translate human-readable domain names (like www.certtest.com) into machine-readable IP addresses. This allows users to access websites using domain names instead of having to remember complex numerical IP addresses.

296. Answer: D

Explanation: DNS operates on Layer 7 of the OSI model, which is the Application Layer. This layer is responsible for high-level services such as web browsing, email, and file transfers.

297. Answer: B

Explanation: DHCP, which stands for Dynamic Host Configuration Protocol, can automatically configure the IP address, subnet mask, and DNS settings on a computer, thus simplifying network management.

298. Answer: B

Explanation: DHCP operates on Layer 2 of the OSI model, which is the Data Link Layer. This layer is responsible for node-to-node data transfer and for detecting and possibly correcting errors that may occur in the Physical Layer.

299. Answer: A

Explanation: While DHCP is convenient for automatically configuring IP settings on user workstations, manual IP configuration is still preferred for network servers to ensure a more stable and secure network environment.

300. Answer: C

Explanation: The text mentions that a major problem with traditional DNS is its lack of security, which can lead to attacks such as DNS poisoning.

301. Answer: D

Explanation: A fully qualified domain name (FQDN) includes both the hostname and the domain name, providing a complete address of a device on the Internet.

302. Answer: B

Explanation: DHCP broadcasts are not passed by routers because routers provide insulation from unnecessary traffic. To overcome this, routers can be configured with DHCP helper addresses, which forward DHCP requests to the appropriate server.

303. Answer: B

Explanation: The text states the Achilles' heel of DHCP is its reliance on broadcasts (using the device's MAC address) to obtain an IP address, which routers do not pass by default.

304. Answer: A

Explanation: The preferred method to enhance DNS security is to implement Secure DNS (S-DNS), which uses access control lists (ACLs) and digital certificates to ensure that name-lookup services and DNS updates are accepted only from verified servers.

305. Answer: A

Explanation: A router with a DHCP-helper-address is configured to forward DHCP requests to a different subnet, allowing for dynamic IP addressing across multiple subnets.

306. Answer: C

Explanation: A router with a WAN port is specifically designed to connect a local area network (LAN) to a remote wide area network (WAN) using telephone circuits.

307. Answer: D

Explanation: X.25 was an early digital packet-switching protocol that laid the groundwork for modern switched networks, including the Internet.

308. Answer: C

Explanation: IPsec VPNs use transport mode when there's no need to hide the sender's or recipient's network address and tunnel mode to conceal both parties' identities by encrypting both the payload and header information.

309. Answer: C

Explanation: The first-generation packet filtering firewall had significant issues with logging and implementing effective granular rules, making it difficult to manage and monitor network traffic efficiently.

310. Answer: B

Explanation: In the context of network firewalls, DMZ stands for Demilitarized Zone. It refers to a screened subnet that is exposed to untrusted networks, typically used to host servers that need to be accessible from the internet.

311. Answer: C

Explanation: IEEE 802.11a/b/g/n standards are considered unsafe due to security vulnerabilities, particularly in their implementations of WEP and WPA encryption methods.

312. Answer: A

Explanation: A multi-layered approach using both host-based IDPS on critical servers, routers, and devices, as well as network-based IDPS on backbone segments and subnets, is recommended to ensure comprehensive monitoring and detection of intrusions.

313. Answer: C

Explanation: A Local Area Network (LAN) is used to connect computers and devices within a single building or closely situated buildings, offering high-speed connections and facilitating communication and resource sharing within a limited geographical area.

314. Answer: C

Explanation: Both early service bureaus and modern SaaS models operate on the concept of relying on someone else's server hardware to process data for users, despite changes in technology and terminology over the years.

315. Answer: C

Explanation: The term "Application Service Provider (ASP)" was introduced by a smart salesperson to make the service bureau concept sound newer and more appealing.

316. Answer: C

Explanation: SaaS offers instant scalability where users can expand or upgrade their services by paying more money, often in the form of subscription fees.

317. Answer: B

Explanation: One advantage of using SaaS is the faster transfer of business to new owners, as it allows for easier management of due diligence and reduces delays in ownership transfer.

318. Answer: A

Explanation: One of the advantages of SaaS is actually the lower initial cost, as the infrastructure is provided by the vendor. Disadvantages include potential high expenses over time, loss of control over data, and liability concerns.

319. Answer: C

Explanation: Public cloud services, such as Google Docs and Facebook, provide shared resources to subscribers, often with free starter usage, and typically have service agreements that exempt the provider from liability for data loss or breaches.

320. Answer: C

Explanation: Private cloud services are often chosen by clients who are concerned about the confidentiality of their data, regulatory data requirements, and want to have control over who accesses their data.

321. Answer: D

Explanation: Cooperative cloud services are where professional associations and community groups may have their computing cloud service. They are a variation of the public cloud service model and are unlikely to involve substantial financial investment or negotiated service levels.

322. Answer: C

Explanation: Subscribers retain liability for any failures when using SaaS or cloud services because they are responsible for their decision to use a third-party vendor, and this is often reinforced by service agreements.

323. Answer: C

Explanation: The principal motivation for using SaaS is to lower the expense of infrastructure and ongoing operating costs, allowing for rapid deployment of applications sometimes without involving the IT department.

324. Answer: C

Explanation: The text explicitly states that the most effective method for reducing operating costs is to improve software automation. By automating tasks, organizations can increase efficiency and reduce the need for manual intervention, which in turn lowers costs.

325. Answer: B

Explanation: The term "risk appetite" is used to refer to the level of risk that an organization is willing to accept in pursuit of its objectives. In this context, it refers to the auditee taking inappropriate shortcuts secretly.

326. Answer: B

Explanation: After the implementation phase, the software enters production use and undergoes ongoing maintenance. This includes a series of patch updates and retesting of system integrity.

327. Answer: A

Explanation: According to the text, 85 percent of a business's functions are related to common clerical office administration tasks, which are usually automated with commercial off-the-shelf software.

328. Answer: C

Explanation: Commercial off-the-shelf software, such as productivity suites like Microsoft Office or Apache OpenOffice, requires little customization and offers small but useful financial advantages to businesses.

329. Answer: C

Explanation: A strategic system is defined in the text as one that fundamentally changes the way the organization conducts business or competes in the marketplace, resulting in significant improvements in overall business performance.

330. Answer: C

Explanation: The text provides auction software implemented and marketed by eBay as an example of a strategic system that fundamentally changes the way an organization is run.

331. Answer: B

Explanation: The text distinguishes a strategic system by its dramatic, measurable results and significant return on investment for the entire organization, as opposed to a tactical system which provides departmental support and may offer a smaller return on investment.

332. Answer: B

Explanation: Auditors are advised to be cautious of software vendors that claim strategic value with obscure results, as these claims might be used to sell lesser products at higher profit margins without delivering true strategic benefits.

333. Answer: C

Explanation: The auditor's role in software development is to determine whether the organizational objectives have been properly identified and met, ensuring that claims of improvement are verifiable.

334. Answer: B

Explanation: CMM Level 1 - Initial is characterized by ad hoc activities, where processes are unstructured and performed by individuals. This level includes prototyping experiments and troubleshooting problems, often with unpredictable results and inconsistent management activities. Decision authority resides in the individual workers and is supported by a local manager.

335. Answer: C

Explanation: CMM Level 2 - Repeatable is the minimum requirement to obtain and maintain ISO 9001 quality certification. This level involves documenting processes in detail with specific procedures that can be repeated consistently.

336. Answer: C

Explanation: At CMM Level 3 - Defined, standardization begins to take place between departments with both qualitative and quantitative measurements. Formal criteria are developed for use in decision selection processes, and decisions are made by formal review committees for the overall good of the business.

337. Answer: C

Explanation: CMM Level 4 - Managed is characterized by quantitative measurement, where numeric measurement of quality is used. Portfolio asset management and a formal project priority system are practiced.

338. Answer: D

Explanation: CMM Level 5 - Optimized represents the highest level of control, focused on continuous improvement using statistical process control. At this level, a culture of constant improvement is pervasive.

339. Answer: D

Explanation: ISO 15504 (SPICE) is a modified version of the CMM that uses slightly different terminology to express the various maturity levels across different languages and cultures. However, the levels correspond closely to those of the CMM.

340. Answer: C

Explanation: The main goal of the CMM is to eliminate decision authority from the department managers and workers, shifting control higher up to the executive management level as process maturity increases.

341. Answer: A

Explanation: In the revised ISO 9001:2015 edition, a shift occurred to allow a risk-based approach, providing room for alternative shortcut methods to reduce costs, while still requiring a formally adopted quality manual.

342. Answer: C

Explanation: ISO 15489:2001 is the standard designed to ensure that adequate records are created, captured, and managed, applying to managing all forms of records and record-keeping policies.

343. Answer: A

Explanation: ISO 9126 defines six quality attributes for evaluating software products: Functionality, Ease of Use (user satisfaction), Reliability, Efficiency, Portability, and Maintainability. These attributes assess the integrity, user satisfaction, consistent performance, resource utilization, environment independence, and ease of modification of software processes.

344. Answer: C

Explanation: The primary purpose of an Executive Steering Committee in the context of software decisions is to provide guidance and ensure that IT functions are aligned with the current business objectives.

345. Answer: B

Explanation: Critical Success Factors (CSFs) are elements that are essential for achieving strategic objectives, and they must go right every time to avoid being a showstopper.

346. Answer: C

Explanation: The most effective decisions from a steering committee are obtained by mutual agreement of the committee members rather than by directive.

347. Answer: C

Explanation: Business needs are established from both internal sources, such as the steering committee and performance metrics, and external sources, such as regulations and competitors.

348. Answer: C

Explanation: A typical RFP contains an overview of the objectives and timeline for the review process, background information about the organization, and a detailed list of requirements.

349. Answer: B

Explanation: The main advantage of using the Scenario Approach is the discovery of assumptions that are no longer relevant and challenging the planning assumptions.

350. Answer: B

Explanation: The role of an IS auditor is to ensure that the proposed system is properly aligned with business requirements and contains the necessary internal controls.

351. Answer: B

Explanation: A key consideration when determining feasibility is ensuring that the right resources are available to implement the proposed system.

352. Answer: A

Explanation: The organization should consider whether commercial software is available to perform the desired functions and what level of customization would be required.

353. Answer: C

Explanation: The main concern is the possibility of vendors responding with a low bid that undercuts the minimum requirements and then overcharging the customer with expensive change orders to meet the stated objectives.

354. Answer: B

Explanation: The Change Control Board is responsible for reviewing all requests for changes and determining whether they should be authorized. This is to ensure that changes are made in a controlled manner and minimize the risk of disruption to the business.

355. Answer: B

Explanation: The chairperson of the Change Control Board is usually someone in a high-level position such as a vice president, director, or senior manager. This reflects the importance of the board's decisions and the need for experienced leadership.

356. Answer: A

Explanation: Input from business users is essential in the change control review process to ensure that the changes meet the business needs and that the impact on users is considered.

357. Answer: A

Explanation: The CCB should weigh each change request by considering the business need, the scope of the change, the level of risk, and what preparations are necessary to prevent failure.

358. Answer: C

Explanation: The enforcement of separation of duties within the change management process can be determined by referring to the client organization's policies concerning change control.

359. Answer: B

Explanation: Every meeting of the Change Control Board should include a complete tracking of current activities and the minutes of the meetings to ensure proper documentation and accountability.

360. Answer: B

Explanation: The ultimate goal of the Change Control Board in managing changes is to prevent business interruption, ensuring that operations continue smoothly despite any changes being made.

361. Answer: A

Explanation: To prevent business interruption, the principles of version control, configuration management, and testing are followed during the change management process.

362. Answer: B

Explanation: The approval process within the Change Control Board should be formal and documented, ensuring a consistent and traceable method of managing changes.

363. Answer: C

Explanation: The text mentions evolutionary and revolutionary as the two opposing viewpoints on managing software development. The evolutionary approach involves significant effort during the planning and design phase and releases software in incremental stages. In contrast, the revolutionary approach empowers business users to develop their own software without a programmer's aid, which is high-risk and does not fit into traditional management techniques.

364. Answer: B

Explanation: According to the evolutionary view, the number-one source of failures in software development is a result of errors in planning and design. This approach emphasizes the importance of thorough planning and design before actual coding begins.

365. Answer: C

Explanation: Evolutionary software is released in incremental stages, starting with a selected module used in the architecture of the first release. Subsequent modules are added to expand features and improve functionality. The software is not considered finished until all increments are completed and assembled.

366. Answer: C

Explanation: The revolutionary development approach is associated with fourth-generation programming languages (4GL), which are designed to allow business users to develop their own software without the need for a trained programmer.

367. Answer: D

Explanation: The revolutionary development approach is difficult to manage because it does not fit into traditional management techniques, lacks internal controls, and there is a significant risk that it may fail to obtain its objectives.

368. Answer: A

Explanation: The text specifies that the Precedence Diagramming Method (PDM) and Critical Path Method (CPM) are advantages used in evolutionary software development. PDM shows the ripple effect of changes to the project, while CPM indicates core priorities.

369. Answer: B

Explanation: The three models used to illustrate the SDLC, as mentioned in the text, are the waterfall model, the spiral model, and the agile prototyping model. Each provides a different perspective on how software development can be approached and managed.

370. Answer: B

Explanation: Boehm's modification of W. W. Royce's waterfall model includes validation testing with backward loops that return to the previous phase, allowing for changes in requirements during development and ensuring these changes do not produce negative consequences.

371. Answer: C

Explanation: The spiral model, proposed by Barry Boehm, is a risk-driven software development process model that emphasizes iterative development and the incremental release of software. It involves multiple cycles or spirals of development, each consisting of four key phases: determining objectives, risk analysis, development, and planning for the next iteration. This iterative approach allows for the creation of evolutionary versions of the software through repeated cycles of development and refinement..

372. Answer: C

Explanation: Agile prototyping is useful when tasks are unpredictable, there is a lack of a detailed plan, or the best design is unknown since it has not undergone initial prototype engineering. Agile fits into the void where a project involves trial and error and learning from mistakes.

373. Answer: C

Explanation: The main focus of Phase 1 in the SDLC is the Feasibility Study. This phase is concerned with determining the strategic benefits that the new system would generate, defining objectives, performing preliminary risk assessment, agreeing on an initial budget and ROI, and identifying market opportunities.

374. Answer: B

Explanation: ERDs and flowcharts are developed during the Requirements Definition phase of the SDLC. This phase involves creating a detailed definition of needs and planning the solution based on objectives and specifications from earlier phases.

375. Answer: C

Explanation: The System Design phase is where a solution or strategy is planned using the objectives from Phase 1 and specifications from Phase 2. It involves creating detailed specifications of internal system design or developing a valid configuration for purchased products.

376. Answer: C

Explanation: The Development phase is where programmers are busy writing the individual lines of program code, building prototypes for functional testing, and performing software testing to ensure everything works as intended.

377. Answer: C

Explanation: The Implementation phase synthesizes the decisions made in previous phases into one functional system that is installed and prepared for final user acceptance testing and training.

378. Answer: C

Explanation: Postimplementation reviews should occur every year the system is in production use, to ensure continuous effectiveness and fulfillment of the original objectives.

379. Answer: C

Explanation: The Disposal phase is the proper shutdown and dismantling of the system, ensuring data is archived and equipment is disposed of in an acceptable manner without profit from the disposal within the organization.

380. Answer: B

Explanation: FPA stands for Function Point Analysis. It is a structured method for classifying the components of a software program and is used to estimate the work required to develop the software.

381. Answer: B

Explanation: System Accreditation is not listed as a phase in the ISACA SDLC. It is a part of the Implementation phase where management accredits the system for specified use after technical certification.

382. Answer: B

Explanation: The Constructive Cost Model (COCOMO) is a forecasting model that estimates the effort, schedule, and cost of developing a new software application. It helps in performing "what if" calculations to show the effect of changes on resources, schedule, staffing, and predicted cost.

383. Answer: D

Explanation: The ACID model for database integrity consists of Atomicity, Consistency, Isolation, and Durability. Flexibility is not a part of the ACID model.

384. Answer: C

Explanation: Atomicity means that a database transaction must be all or nothing—if a transaction fails, any changes made are backed out, and the database is restored to its original state.

385. Answer: B

Explanation: Foreign keys are used to link tables together in a data-oriented database, establishing a relationship between an item of data in one table and data contained in a separate table.

386. Answer: C

Explanation: The main advantage of OODB is the combination of data and program methods into objects, which allows for greater flexibility and modularity, especially when dealing with data of an unpredictable nature.

387. Answer: C

Explanation: The term 'key' in databases is used to illustrate the concept that certain data items, like primary keys, candidate keys, and foreign keys, are necessary to unlock or access related information in a database.

388. Answer: C

Explanation: Referential integrity is a property of data that ensures that relationships between tables remain consistent, such that keys referenced across different tables are valid and correspond correctly to each other.

389. Answer: C

Explanation: In the context of databases, 'attributes' are synonymous with columns in a table, which hold specific pieces of data within the table's structure.

390. Answer: C

Explanation: A 'tuple' is a term used by computer programmers to refer to a row in a database table, which is a record consisting of multiple fields.

391. Answer: A

Explanation: When a transaction is 'committed' in a database, it means that the changes made during the transaction are permanently written to the master file, and the transaction is then deleted from the journals.

392. Answer: A

Explanation: Data normalization is the process used in a data-oriented structured database to standardize and remove duplicates, which helps to minimize redundancy and improve search efficiency.

393. Answer: C

Explanation: The primary purpose of a DSS is to provide senior-level managers with timely information that assists them in making effective decisions. It serves as a tool to support, not replace, the decision-making process by presenting relevant information.

394. Answer: B

Explanation: Data Mining is the process in which the DSS drills down through the data to find correlations that may represent answers or insights.

395. Answer: B

Explanation: The data warehouse's job is to combine data from various systems, which aids in providing a comprehensive view for decision-making purposes.

396. Answer: B

Explanation: A data mart is a repository that holds data mining results from the data warehouse and serves like a convenience store for the most common data requests.

397. Answer: C

Explanation: A DSS typically uses a Graphical User Interface (GUI) to display prepackaged results of data mining for the user, making it easier to interpret the data.

398. Answer: B

Explanation: Heuristic program rules in a DSS may be based on fuzzy logic, which uses estimation, means, and averages to calculate likely outcomes.

399. Answer: C

Explanation: Senior executives benefit the most from the information presented by the data mart, as it aids them in detecting upcoming trends or areas of concern within the organization.

400. Answer: C

Explanation: Artificial Intelligence (AI) is the next step up from DSSs, as it involves computers evolving to a level where they can make their own decisions, potentially without human intervention. AI is particularly useful for machines operating in hostile environments requiring immediate autonomous responses.

401. Answer: C

Explanation: An open system architecture is based on well-known standards and definitions, allowing for flexibility, as computer software can be updated and modified using components from multiple sources.

402. Answer: C

Explanation: The primary advantage of open architecture is its flexibility and the ability to use components from multiple sources to use best-of-breed programs.

403. Answer: C

Explanation: A closed system architecture contains methods and proprietary programming that remain the property of the software creator, with most of the program logic hidden from view or encrypted.

404. Answer: C

Explanation: Most commercial software products are closed, proprietary systems but with industry standardized program interfaces for data sharing with other programs, essentially being closed architecture with open architecture interfaces.

405. Answer: B

Explanation: One advantage of closed system architecture for vendors is the ability to lock in customers to their product, which can create a steady customer base for the vendor.

406. Answer: C

Explanation: A disadvantage for customers using closed system architecture software is the potential of being locked into the vendor's product, limiting their options for other software solutions.

407. Answer: B

Explanation: In the context of a DSS, a data warehouse is a storage for data snapshots and typically involves separate databases that contain un-normalized data.

408. Answer: B

Explanation: A data mart is essentially a subset of a data warehouse that is designed to cater to the needs of specific users or user groups, focusing on a particular subject or department.

409. Answer: B

Explanation: 'Cleaning and mining' refer to the process of removing redundancies and researching correlations in the context of data warehouses, which is essential for ensuring the quality and usability of the data for decision-making purposes.

410. Answer: C

Explanation: Organizations must decide whether to use a centralized database, which is easier to manage, or a distributed database application, which offers more flexibility and redundancy. This is a significant challenge because it impacts the management, flexibility, and security of the organization's data.

411. Answer: C

Explanation: A centralized database system is easier to manage compared to a distributed system. This is because all data is stored in a single location, which simplifies administration and maintenance tasks.

412. Answer: C

Explanation: Distributed database systems offer more flexibility and redundancy. They allow data to be stored across multiple locations, which can prevent total data loss in case of a failure at one site and provide more options for scaling and managing the data.

413. Answer: B

Explanation: The distributed database system carries higher implementation and support costs due to its complexity, the need for managing multiple systems, and the increased number of support decisions that can lead to security failures.

414. Answer: B

Explanation: Centralized systems facilitate mandatory access controls by eliminating local data access decisions, thus centralizing the authority and control over who or what can interact with the data.

415. Answer: C

Explanation: Decentralized systems increase the number of support decisions, which in turn increases the complexity of the security infrastructure and the likelihood of a security failure due to potential inconsistencies or errors in decision-making.

416. Answer: B

Explanation: The decision of centralization versus decentralization is typically addressed in Phase 2 of the SDLC, which is the Requirements Definition phase. During this phase, the requirements for systems such as electronic commerce are gathered and analyzed.

417. Answer: C

Explanation: The specific requirements for electronic commerce, such as scalability, reliability, and security, would influence the decision between using a centralized or a distributed database system.

418. Answer: C

Explanation: Decentralized systems are less likely to feature simplified management because they involve managing data across multiple locations, which can complicate administration and support tasks.

419. Answer: D

Explanation: Increased support decisions in decentralized systems imply greater administrative complexity for the organization. This is because each decision point can introduce variability and potential security risks that need to be managed.

420. Answer: A

Explanation: E-commerce stands for Electronic Commerce, which involves conducting business and financial transactions electronically across the globe.

421. Answer: D

Explanation: Consumer-to-Consumer (C2C) is not mentioned in the provided text as a type of e-commerce transaction. The mentioned types are B2B, B2G, B2C, and Business-to-Employee (B2E).

422. Answer: C

Explanation: B2B transactions occur between a business and its vendors, involving purchasing, accounts payable, payroll, and outsourcing services.

423. Answer: D

Explanation: Business-to-Employee (B2E) transactions, including online employee service administration, are governed by federal employment and privacy regulations.

424. Answer: D

Explanation: Business-to-government transactions are governed by a variety of government regulations, such as online filing of legal documents and reports, as well as purchasing and vendor management for products and services used by the government.

425. Answer: B

Explanation: Vendors doing business with the US government are required to maintain their company profiles in the US Central Contractor Registration (CCR) database.

426. Answer: C

Explanation: Business-to-Consumer (B2C) transactions include direct sales of products and services to consumers as well as providing customer support and product information.

427. Answer: B

Explanation: Business-to-consumer applications require additional logging to compensate for the absence of the normal paper trail associated with traditional transactions.

428. Answer: A

Explanation: Authorizations for processing online payments in B2C transactions require special security measures, including strong internal controls due to the level of risk involved.

429. Answer: D

Explanation: Business-to-Employee (B2E) transactions include the online administration of employee services, such as payroll and job benefits, and are governed by federal regulations and privacy laws.

430. Answer: C

Explanation: IT is often viewed as a cost center and is not perceived to face the same pressures as business units, which is a point of disconnect between IT and the rest of the organization. The text describes IT as closed up and isolated, not facing the business pressures that other units do.

431. Answer: C

Explanation: The principal reason for IT outsourcing is the lack of intricate knowledge of how each business unit operates, which leads to the perception that IT is not fully integrated with the rest of the business.

432. Answer: B

Explanation: The first common statement about improving IT operations mentioned in the text is "Buy More," which suggests that buying new products is seen as a solution.

433. Answer: C

Explanation: The third choice that gets closer to the real solution is committing resources to document and measure the current situation to determine the root of the problems.

434. Answer: A

Explanation: IT governance deals with executives recognizing their responsibility, taking control of IT issues, making educated decisions, and acting on them.

435. Answer: B

Explanation: The first objective of IT leadership mentioned is to define IT's mission using simple words and then set out plans to accomplish it.

436. Answer: B

Explanation: The perception of IT is suggested to change by transforming the image of IT staff from blue-jeans-wearing introverts to organized, sharp-looking professionals who support critical business aspects.

437. Answer: D

Explanation: External measures are from the customer viewpoint and include system availability, perception of the help desk, response time, and overall customer satisfaction.

438. Answer: B

Explanation: Internal measures are of interest to systems people in IT and involve technical details such as availability, disk storage capacity, and service requests.

439. Answer: C

Explanation: The objective of shifting change control is to move from the needs of IT toward aligning with the specific business objectives of the users in other departments.

440. Answer: B

Explanation: IT Operations Managers are responsible for managing a team that covers a broad range of IT functions, including software development, help desk support, server and network administration, and overseeing information security measures.

441. Answer: C

Explanation: ITIL is the framework that offers a comprehensive set of management practices designed to guide help desk operations in delivering high-quality IT services.

442. Answer: B

Explanation: The Systems Architect reviews information from the systems analyst and determines the preferred design for new systems, creating the overall system layout.

443. Answer: A

Explanation: ITIL's service support function includes service desk operations, incident management, and problem management, focusing on the day-to-day interaction with the end-users.

444. Answer: B

Explanation: IT Operations Management aims to support the daily operational needs of business users, ensuring that the technology is effective and aligns with business objectives.

445. Answer: C

Explanation: ISSAs are responsible for collaborating with various departments to enhance security measures, conduct awareness training, and help test security settings.

446. Answer: B

Explanation: Lights-out operations refer to an unmanned facility where control room or data center operations are either fully automated or run by remote control, significantly reducing risks associated with human error or presence.

447. Answer: B

Explanation: An SLA is designed to create an understanding between the service provider and the user, detailing the quality and quantity of service expected.

448. Answer: B

Explanation: IT asset management is focused on maintaining control over the organization's digital assets, which includes data and software licenses, ensuring proper governance and monitoring for usage violations.

449. Answer: B

Explanation: The Media Librarian is tasked with the critical role of tracking all media, ensuring its safe storage, and managing the data's tracking history, including offsite storage arrangements.

450. Answer: B

Explanation: Capacity management primarily focuses on the process of monitoring existing computing resources to track their usage and planning accordingly for their future availability to ensure that the resources can handle upcoming demands.

451. Answer: B

Explanation: IT administrators utilize system-monitoring tools to gauge computing resources' current state and make reasonable estimates of the system capacity needed for future operations.

452. Answer: B

Explanation: System utilization reports are instrumental in providing detailed information about the current processing workload, which can be used to assess system performance and forecast future capacity needs.

453. Answer: B

Explanation: External changes, such as modifications in service-level agreements or variations in the number of users, can directly impact the available capacity of computing resources.

454. Answer: C

Explanation: Cloud services provide on-demand availability, which discourages clients from needing to plan ahead for capacity, as the resources are designed to be scalable and readily available as per the client's requirements.

455. Answer: C

Explanation: It is often inevitable that a few single points of failure will exist within a system, either because of the technology selected or due to the financial implications of establishing complete redundancy.

456. Answer: C

Explanation: Duplicate firewalls, when set up to share the workload in parallel, can double the available capacity by providing two independent communication paths, thereby enhancing the system's ability to handle traffic.

457. Answer: C

Explanation: When duplicate firewalls share the workload in parallel, it results in two independent communication paths, which can improve network reliability and capacity by allowing traffic to be evenly distributed between them.

458. Answer: B

Explanation: The primary objective of information security management is to protect computing resources by ensuring their confidentiality, integrity, and availability. This includes implementing organizational designs that support security objectives and managing known, unknown, and adversary-created vulnerabilities.

459. Answer: C

Explanation: The Chief Information Security Officer (CISO) is the role developed to have the highest level of authority over information systems security. The CISO's main responsibility is to define and enforce the organization's security policies.

460. Answer: A

Explanation: Without an information classification scheme, there is a risk of mishandling information, which can lead to inappropriate destruction or leaks. Additionally, in the absence of such a scheme, all organizational data may be subject to scrutiny during legal proceedings, which can lead to loss of sensitive or confidential data.

461. Answer: C

Explanation: A Data Custodian is responsible for implementing the controls necessary to safeguard data and ensuring its availability to authorized users. The custodian's duties include monitoring security, administering access controls, ensuring data integrity, and backing up data to prevent loss.

462. Answer: B

Explanation: Documenting physical access paths is crucial for ensuring accountability for record-keeping and risk assessment integrity. It helps identify known access routes, a prerequisite for internal controls and security.

463. Answer: B

Explanation: The Chief Privacy Officer (CPO) is responsible for the protection of confidential information of clients and employees. The CPO ensures that privacy laws and regulations are complied with and that personal data is handled appropriately.

464. Answer: B

Explanation: The information classification process is used to define the level of controls necessary to ensure the appropriate confidentiality, integrity, and availability based on the value, sensitivity, content, and context of the information.

465. Answer: B

Explanation: Data retention requirements are based on several factors, including the value of the data, its useful life, and legal requirements that dictate how long certain types of records must be retained before they are archived or disposed of.

466. Answer: C

Explanation: Software licenses represent a major capital investment and are viewed as assets of the corporation that require effective control and management. Organizations need to manage them to ensure copyright compliance and avoid legal and financial penalties.

467. Answer: D

Explanation: Compensating controls are alternative methods that are used when a preferred control cannot be implemented. They are collections of less effective controls that work together to provide similar protection to mitigate the impact of errors or omissions.

468. Answer: C

Explanation: The first phase in the incident response life cycle is Preparation, which includes appointing team members, getting the team trained, and providing the necessary procedures and tools to perform the job effectively.

469. Answer: C

Explanation: Scheduled IT maintenance reports are not typically a source for detecting incidents. Instead, system log reports, telephone calls to the help desk, and constant IT monitoring are cited as primary sources of detection.

470. Answer: C

Explanation: The role of an IS auditor in personnel management is to ascertain if proper controls are in place to manage the activities of people within the organization.

471. Answer: B

Explanation: The purpose of problem management in IT operations is to deliver a timely response to issues by utilizing predefined procedures, including a method for problem escalation.

472. Answer: B

Explanation: When a violation of the Acceptable Use Policy is discovered, it should trigger the incident-handling process and notification to human resources.

473. Answer: B

Explanation: If a computer processing job ends too fast, it may indicate that a portion of the processing was skipped, which could signify a substantial problem.

474. Answer: C

Explanation: The Incident Response Team's role is to analyze and respond to security incidents. They are activated when an incident is detected to limit the damage and manage the situation.

475. Answer: B

Explanation: Implementing preventative controls, such as properly maintained antivirus software, can save money by reducing the occurrence of problems.

476. Answer: B

Explanation: The acquisition phase of the forensic life cycle deals with acquiring data from the best possible sources, including recovering data from deleted files and creating bitstream images of the original media.

477. Answer: B

Explanation: Before starting a digital forensic investigation, auditors and investigators should obtain a clear, written mandate from the appropriate authority, indicating that they have lawful authorization to proceed.

478. Answer: B

Explanation: System monitoring is essential in IT service delivery as it helps to uncover operational inconsistencies, errors, and processing failures. By continuously monitoring the system, the system administrator can be aware of the hardware conditions, reported problems, and alerts recorded in system logs, thereby allowing for proactive IT infrastructure management and ensuring system availability.

479. Answer: C

Explanation: Event logs and audit logs should be enabled and configured to capture information of interest, including error conditions, successful logins, unsuccessful login attempts, and configuration changes. These logs play a vital role in security monitoring and incident response, providing a record of activity that can be analyzed to detect and respond to potential security threats.

480. Answer: B

Explanation: SCAP stands for Security Content Automation Protocol, and it is used to verify the system's security state by rechecking the status of modifications. SCAP can relock settings or notify of unauthorized modifications, indicating a potential attack in progress, thereby enhancing an organization's security posture.

481. Answer: C

Explanation: The recommended practice for centralized system logging is to have a process that forwards a copy of each system log to a centralized console for review. This setup, along with a log-reading tool, helps convert raw data into meaningful information and effectively manages the volume of log entries.

482. Answer: D

Explanation: According to the text, there are only two categories of uptime-downtime reporting: Uptime, where the system is available for users to process data, and Downtime, where the system is unavailable for any reason, including failure or a scheduled outage for service. Partial uptime is not mentioned as a category and does not fit the clear distinction between uptime and downtime described in the text.

483. Answer: C

Explanation: Logical access includes the invisible layers of electronics and software that operate in unison as one combined system within a computer. This encompasses aspects such as ingress, egress, default settings, and shared administrative access, which are critical for maintaining system security.

484. Answer: B

Explanation: The principle of 'least privilege' means that no individual should have access to IT computing resources beyond what their job requires. By implementing this principle, organizations can minimize the risk of unauthorized access or damage, as users only have the necessary access rights to perform their duties.

485. Answer: B

Explanation: When the organization no longer employs a user, their account needs to be suspended or disabled upon notice from HR. A critical step before the deletion of the user ID is to conduct an administrative review to check for unauthorized access attempts. If there are no issues, the user's data files should be archived and forwarded to the appropriate department manager.

486. Answer: B

Explanation: Maintenance login accounts, which often have well-known and commercially published login IDs, should be disabled in a production system to prevent unauthorized access. If necessary, any valid maintenance accounts should use non-typical login names with strong passwords or station restrictions to enhance security.

487. Answer: C

Explanation: Application processing controls are designed to assure system security and integrity by providing internal processing controls within each application. These controls include input, processing, and output controls which ensure that data is entered, processed, and output securely and accurately, maintaining the integrity of the system.

488. Answer: D

Explanation: Traditional tumbler locks are relatively inexpensive and easy to install, but their major drawback is that everyone uses the same key to open the lock, making it impossible to identify who exactly has accessed the lock at any given time.

489. Answer: C

Explanation: Closed-circuit television can be used for real-time monitoring of access routes and can also provide audit logs of past activity, which is important to check for events that might have occurred days or weeks ago.

490. Answer: B

Explanation: Higher-security cipher locks issue a unique code for each individual, improving security by ensuring access is personalized and more easily audited.

491. Answer: C

Explanation: Gas chemical systems are frequently used in computer installations because they avoid the hazards created by water. These systems use an inert gas like FM-200 to extinguish fires.

492. Answer: C

Explanation: The EPO switch is designed to quickly kill power in the event of an emergency to prevent electrocution and other hazards.

493. Answer: B

Explanation: The offsite storage facility should be secure, bonded, and designed for protection against flood, fire, and theft. It should also have 24-hour security and not be visibly marked in a way that would attract attention to the sensitive data stored within.

494. Answer: B

Explanation: Wire cable trays protect cables from water, physical abrasion, and accidental disruption, ensuring safety and uninterrupted operation. It is a standard in professional installations according to EIA/TIA standards.

495. Answer: B

Explanation: Improper disposal of hard drives without data destruction can lead to data recovery, which risks exposing sensitive information. Methods like overwriting, degaussing, or physical destruction should be used to prevent this.

496. Answer: B

Explanation: While manual power transfer switches can be part of the power backup strategy, relying solely on them is not recommended because it does not allow for automatic switching between power sources in the event of an outage. Automated switching with manual override is the better practice.

497. Answer: B

Explanation: The text compares the use of a secret tunnel for emissaries to enter and exit a castle fortress in secret with the use of a Virtual Private Network (VPN) in the modern day to accomplish confidential access.

498. Answer: C

Explanation: Confidentiality is created by implementing rigid data classification and separation of duties in administrative functions, physical characteristics, and electronic technical processes.

499. Answer: C

Explanation: An ethical hacker, also known as a white-hat hacker, is authorized to test computer security defenses to identify weaknesses.

500. Answer: B

Explanation: Social engineering is an active attack where the attacker uses deception to manipulate individuals into breaking normal security procedures. Eavesdropping, host traffic analysis, and network analysis are passive attacks focused on observation and gathering information.

501. Answer: B

Explanation: Spear phishing is a more targeted version that focuses on specific individuals or systems to manipulate them into revealing confidential information.

502. Answer: C

Explanation: The text highlights that an employee within the organization has more access and opportunity to sensitive information and systems than anyone else, and thus, they pose the greatest internal threat through betrayal.

503. Answer: B

Explanation: A zero-day attack refers to an attack that takes advantage of a vulnerability on the day it is discovered before developers have a chance to fix it or issue a patch.

504. Answer: C

Explanation: Internal firewalls are implemented to block attacks and provide a security barrier that protects against threats originating both outside and inside the organization.

505. Answer: B

Explanation: A logic bomb is a type of malicious software that remains dormant within a system until a specific trigger event occurs, at which point it activates and carries out its intended malicious function.

506. Answer: C

Explanation: MAC uses labels to identify the security classification of data and determines access through a set of rules and the comparison of security labels. This ensures that only the right subject can access the right object when all security labels match.

507. Answer: A

Explanation: DAC does not use labels to determine access; this is a characteristic of Mandatory Access Control (MAC). DAC allows the data owner to determine access control at their discretion using permissions like read (r), write (w), and execute (x).

508. Answer: B

Explanation: RBAC grants access based on the user's job role, providing them with the necessary level of access to fulfill their job duties.

509. Answer: B

Explanation: A smart card is an example of Type 2 authentication, where a unique item in the user's possession, combined with knowledge like a PIN, is used to authenticate the user.

510. Answer: C

Explanation: Biometrics uses an individual's unique physical (like fingerprints or iris patterns) or behavioral (like signature dynamics or voice patterns) characteristics to authenticate their identity.

511. Answer: B

Explanation: The purpose of encryption is not to prevent availability but to ensure confidentiality and, when used with digital signatures, to authenticate a user's identity and ensure data integrity.

512. Answer: B

Explanation: A digital certificate contains the owner's public key and identifying information such as their name and contact detail

513. Answer: A

Explanation: A CA is responsible for issuing digital certificates after verifying the identity of the requestor, thereby vouching for the authenticity of the user's email address, which is used to establish a trusted connection between users.

514. Answer: B

Explanation: The CSR is emailed to the Certificate Authority, not the recipient. The CA then uses the CSR to issue a digital certificate for the requester's computer.

515. Answer: B

Explanation: DRM is used to control the use of digital content and protect it from unauthorized access and distribution by embedding special code into the file to ensure it can only be accessed by authorized systems.

516. Answer: B

Explanation: The text suggests that business continuity can be seen as a modern evolution of executive scenario planning, emphasizing the need for businesses to constantly adapt and remain in motion, similar to a shark in the ocean, to survive in a competitive environment.

517. Answer: C

Explanation: The text outlines that executives are generally faced with two choices when under financial pressure: increase revenue or cut costs. These are the primary strategies for maintaining or improving financial performance.

518. Answer: C

Explanation: The text equates handling a 30 percent surge in business with managing a 30 percent reduction in capability, suggesting that both scenarios require significant adaptation and management skills.

519. Answer: B

Explanation: The text states that the primary goal of IT is to make records accessible to the business unit whenever needed, highlighting the importance of information availability.

520. Answer: C

Explanation: The text explains that the business economies in New Orleans and Las Vegas crashed due to external events—a hurricane and a presidential speech, respectively—that had severe impacts on the local economy.

521. Answer: A

Explanation: The text debunks the myth that heavy investments in a business's facility are crucial, suggesting that such investments may actually limit options rather than solve problems.

522. Answer: B

Explanation: The text places greater importance on the skilled business unit staff and their unique knowledge and customer relationships over IT systems, which can be outsourced.

523. Answer: C

Explanation: The text mentions that Wall Street analysts tend to react negatively, urging investors to sell when key executives depart from a company, indicating the importance of key personnel to investor confidence.

524. Answer: C

Explanation: The text emphasizes the advantage of business mobility, which allows a company to adapt to various situations, such as economic constraints, new geographic opportunities, or the aftermath of disasters.

525. Answer: C

Explanation: The text leads to the realization that protecting the individuals who possess critical knowledge and access to important records is paramount, more so than location, technology, or specific vendors.

526. Answer: C

Explanation: The primary objective of Business "Revenue" Continuity (BC) is to ensure an uninterrupted stream of revenue or funding. This is crucial for organizations as they rely on revenue or funding to survive, providing them with time and options.

527. Answer: B

Explanation: Continuity of Operations (COOP) focuses on the goal of continuing uninterrupted operations and can include the context of operating without funding. This is typical for essential services like electricity and telephone providers.

528. Answer: C

Explanation: Emergency Management (EM) is concerned with halting normal operations, shutting down utilities, and evacuating people to save lives.

529. Answer: B

Explanation: A significant risk to business operations under Continuity of Government (COG) is that government officials can commandeer all available resources, which can affect business operations severely.

530. Answer: D

Explanation: Disaster Recovery (DR) is most associated with the process of rebuilding what was damaged to its previous condition or absorbing the impact of damage, which is often the focus of government recovery organizations like FEMA.

531. Answer: B

Explanation: The CFO (Chief Financial Officer) is the executive role most likely to focus on scenario forecasts and financial controls. This role is involved with internal spending controls and decisions to build, fix, or sell off assets.

532. Answer: B

Explanation: During a disaster or state of emergency, the federal government of the affected country will direct an agency, often with the aid of the military, to take charge of protection and control.

533. Answer: B

Explanation: During a crisis, businesses and homes might be evacuated, and the government can commandeer supplies and resources to aid during the emergency.

534. Answer: B

Explanation: Insurance policies normally exclude payment for situations where the government commands resources, which means the owner might not be compensated or might receive compensation much later.

535. Answer: D

Explanation: The CIO (Chief Information Officer) is primarily concerned with the continuity of operations and protecting business records, ensuring that operations can be restored or rebuilt as necessary.

536. Answer: B

Explanation: The primary focus of disaster recovery during the 1980s was on rebuilding after a natural disaster. It was about restoring facilities and salvaging equipment to their pre-disaster state.

537. Answer: B

Explanation: DRI was founded in 1988 using information from FEMA to aid organizations in their disaster recovery planning by providing reference materials.

538. Answer: C

Explanation: Traditional disaster recovery plans lacked the focus on maintaining a steady stream of revenue during the recovery period, which is essential for an organization's survival.

539. Answer: B

Explanation: Financial challenges such as breaching contracts, banking issues, investor sell-offs, client hesitations, and suspended services from business partners can structurally weaken an organization and lead to its halt.

540. Answer: C

Explanation: A reduction in profit margins due to increased operating costs or a decline in sales can rapidly turn a profitable business into an unprofitable one.

541. Answer: C

Explanation: Frontier Airlines had to file for bankruptcy after its credit card processor, First Data, began withholding 100 percent of charge transactions in reserve, causing an economic disaster for the company.

542. Answer: D

Explanation: For an organization's survival, it's crucial to have the CEO or COO lead both business continuity (BC) and disaster recovery (DR) planning to ensure cross-departmental coordination and overcome internal politics.

543. Answer: C

Explanation: Customers and investors are not interested in waiting through long delays after a disaster. Lack of sales during rebuilding can lead them to abandon the organization and invest elsewhere.

544. Answer: B

Explanation: The Frontier Airlines brand name reverted to the public domain after eight years of disuse and was later adopted by a new airline started by former executives of the original Frontier Airlines.

545. Answer: B

Explanation Business continuity planning emphasizes maintaining the public image and ensuring the survival of the organization's brand and investors, which is crucial for the organization's continued existence after a disaster.

546. Answer: B

Explanation: The main purpose of a business continuity plan is to maintain the flow of an organization's core business functions with minimal or no interruption. This involves making sure that the organization can survive and continue generating revenue even in the face of disruptions.

547. Answer: B

Explanation: US Airways experienced a significant software problem that led to a logistical nightmare during peak travel time. This resulted in lost sales and increased operating costs, ultimately leading investors to abandon the airline. America West Airlines took over US Airways for a fraction of its value.

548. Answer: D

Explanation: The Steak and Ale Restaurant Group decided to close all corporate-owned stores on the same day due to overwhelming market pressures and competition. Instead of trying to resurrect the business, they chose to use all remaining funds to pay dividends to stockholders.

549. Answer: B

Explanation: A well-crafted business continuity plan can demonstrate an organization's preparedness and ability to fulfill commitments, which can attract better financial terms from investors and more clients due to increased confidence in the company's stability and reliability.

550. Answer: C

Explanation: An organization that can demonstrate the ability to continue operations despite facing challenges such as delivery problems, negative media image, or disasters can gain a competitive advantage in the marketplace.

551. Answer: B

Explanation: Following the 1906 California earthquake, while other banks were closed to prevent a run on the banks, the Bank of Italy set up temporary operations in a wooden horse cart at the wharf, making loans to help people rebuild and accepting new deposits, which greatly contributed to their growth and eventual rebranding as Bank of America.

552. Answer: B

Explanation: In the event of a surge in business, executing a business continuity plan allows an organization to manage the increased demand by shedding low-profit tasks and ensuring that resources are focused on handling the surge, maintaining business operations, and satisfying customer needs.

553. Answer: B

Explanation: FedEx and UPS were involved in a competition for expansion in which they purchased retail chains to increase the number of their drop-off locations. UPS acquired Office Depot and MailBoxes etc., while FedEx purchased Kinko's.

554. Answer: B

Explanation: The documents produced during the business continuity planning process, which include a current risk analysis and detailed business process blueprints, can be incredibly valuable for various business activities such as licensing, expansion, reorganization, and outsourcing of operations.

555. Answer: C

Explanation: Business continuity is described as a double-sided plan that protects what a business already has and provides opportunities to generate more revenue than ever before. It is a comprehensive strategy that prepares a business to continue operations with fewer resources during disasters and also to exploit market opportunities.

556. Answer: A

Explanation: Business continuity planning is frequently led by an organization's Chief Operating Officer or the Program Management Office. These entities are responsible for integrating smaller departmental plans to create a cohesive strategy.

557. Answer: A

Explanation: Running disaster recovery as an ongoing program of operations is more likely to be successful. Task proficiency is achieved through actual use and practice, and an ongoing program suggests active governance and regular attention to the DR plan.

558. Answer: B

Explanation: Most governments, including the US DRI (Disaster Recovery Institute), and the International Business Continuity Institute (BCI) are primarily focused on emergency management and disaster-related preparation.

559. Answer: A

Explanation: For the success of a BC/DR plan, it's essential to limit coverage to only the highest-value processes. The key to success is prioritizing and protecting the most critical aspects of the business.

560. Answer: C

Explanation: A good BC plan will integrate with the supply-chain plans of business partners, suppliers, clients, and government agencies. This creates a network of reliance and support for critical functions.

561. Answer: C

Explanation: Monthly practice testing and training indicates proper governance in BC/DR planning. Regular activities demonstrate that the organization is actively managing its BC/DR plan.

562. Answer: C

Explanation: Auditors should pay extra attention to tasks that are seldom performed. Infrequent attention to critical tasks increases the risk of failure and is of high interest during an audit.

563. Answer: B

Explanation: The number one priority in business continuity is the customer and the customer interface. Without customers, there is no revenue, and without revenue, business continuity would be difficult or impossible.

564. Answer: B

Explanation: The primary goal of a business continuity program is to ensure the organization survives significant disruptions, including potentially drastic measures such as divesting business units or downsizing staff.

565. Answer: C

Explanation: In the initial phase, securing a detailed risk assessment report is not listed as an objective to secure. The objectives include securing a sponsor, a charter, a defined scope, and specific business objectives.

566. Answer: C

Explanation: Allocation of unlimited funding is not mentioned as a component provided by executive management during the first phase. The components include active leadership participation, identification of the first target, and the establishment of a BC leadership council.

567. Answer: B

Explanation: CSF stands for Critical Success Factor, which represents an objective or task that must be accomplished correctly every single time for the business to succeed.

568. Answer: A

Explanation: KGIs identify the organization's goals and define the individual goals in the workflow. They are used to determine whether the goal will be reached according to forecasts.

569. Answer: B

Explanation: During the discovery process, the Business Impact Analysis (BIA) is most concerned with identifying the company's sequence of steps and timing for its business processes.

570. Answer: C

Explanation: RPO stands for Recovery Point Objective, which defines the level of recovery for a particular item, indicating how much data loss is acceptable in case of disruption.

571. Answer: D

Explanation: Blue Site is not a type of alternate processing location mentioned in BC planning. The mentioned types are Redundant Site, Hot Site, and Cold Site.

572. Answer: A

Explanation Maximum Acceptable Outage (MAO) is the maximum time the systems can be offline before breaching a deadline or causing damage to the organization.

573. Answer: B

Explanation: The External Agency Team is responsible for coordinating with fire, police, FEMA, the FBI, and other government agencies during a business continuity incident.

574. Answer: C

Explanation: An IS auditor's job is to determine how well the objectives of a BC/DR plan have been served by management. This involves evaluating the effectiveness of the plan rather than designing, approving, or implementing it.

575. Answer: B

Explanation: An IS auditor should compare the results of the business impact analysis (BIA) and the workflow-based risk assessment to the various strategies selected for each activity in the overall process timeline to see if they support management's strategy.

576. Answer: C

Explanation: Time delays are critical because they can prevent an organization from recovering data in sufficient time to meet established recovery time objectives (RTOs), which are crucial for the continuity of business operations.

577. Answer: B

Explanation: A 0- to 100-hour timeline document is significant because it outlines the order and prioritizes the recovery process, which is a powerful statement in favor of the client's preparedness for a disaster.

578. Answer: C

Explanation: Manual methods are usually proposed to handle work backlogs when processing capability is significantly diminished due to their low cost. However, substantial testing is required to prove the organization's ability to keep up with the work volume manually.

579. Answer: B

Explanation: A well-organized vital records inventory suggests that the organization is prepared for a successful recovery. An audit can reveal how well-prepared the vital records are for such an event.

580. Answer: C

Explanation: BC/DR plans must be exercised regularly to remain effective. This ensures the plan is up-to-date and the team is familiar with the procedures.

581. Answer: B

Explanation: Reviewing the exercise plan, the results, and the schedule of future exercises would provide valuable insights into how well the organization is preparing for potential disasters and its commitment to continuous improvement of the BC/DR plan.

582. Answer: B

Explanation: Ensuring that the organization has the necessary hardware and skills to recover data in sufficient time is vital for establishing well-founded and realistic recovery time objectives (RTOs).

About Our Products

Other products from VERSAtile Reads are:

Elevate Your Leadership: The 10 Must-Have Skills

Elevate Your Leadership: 8 Effective Communication Skills

Elevate Your Leadership: 10 Leadership Styles for Every Situation

300+ PMP Practice Questions Aligned with PMBOK 7, Agile Methods, and Key Process Groups – 2024

Exam-Cram Essentials Last-Minute Guide to Ace the PMP Exam - Your Express Guide featuring PMBOK® Guide

Career Mastery Blueprint - Strategies for Success in Work and Business

Memory Magic: Unraveling the Secret of Mind Mastery

The Success Equation Psychological Foundations For Accomplishment

Fairy Dust Chronicles – The Short and Sweet of Wonder

B2B Breakthrough – Proven Strategies from Real-World Case Studies

CISSP Fast Track Master: CISSP Essentials for Exam Success

 CISA Fast Track Master: CISA Essentials for Exam Success